INTRODUCTION

This Snapshot guide, excerpted from my guidebook *Rick Steves France*, focuses on Normandy—a fascinating region that teems with turning points. For more than a thousand years, legendary figures such as William the Conqueror, Joan of Arc, and General Dwight D. Eisenhower have changed history here. But Normandy is more than invasions and D-Day beaches. Honfleur's gentle harbor inspired the Impressionists, as did Rouen's magnificent cathedral. A thousand-year-old tapestry in Bayeux captures the drama of medieval warfare in a million stitches. On your journey, discover the architectural—and spiritual—marvel of Mont St. Michel, rising above the tidal flats like a mirage.

To help you have the best trip possible, I've included the following topics in this book:

• **Planning Your Time,** with advice on how to make the most of your limited time

• **Orientation,** including tourist information (abbreviated as TI), tips on public transportation, local tour options, and helpful hints

• **Sights** with ratings:

    ▲▲▲—Don't miss

    ▲▲—Try hard to see

    ▲—Worthwhile if you can make it

    No rating—Worth knowing about

• **Sleeping and Eating,** with good-value recommendations in every price range

• **Connections,** with tips on trains, buses, and driving

Practicalities, near the end of this book, has information on money, staying connected, hotel reservations, transportation, and more, plus French survival phrases.

To travel smartly, read this little book in its entirety before you go. It's my hope that this guide will make your trip more meaningful and rewarding. Traveling like a temporary local, you'll get the absolute most out of every mile, minute, and dollar.

Bon voyage!

Rick Steves

NORMANDY

Rouen • Honfleur • Bayeux • D-Day Beaches
• Mont St-Michel

Sweeping coastlines, half-timbered towns, fortified farmsteads, and thatched roofs decorate the rolling green hills of Normandy (Normandie). Parisians call Normandy "the 21st arrondissement." It's their escape—the nearest beach. Brits consider this area close enough for a weekend away (you'll notice that the BBC comes through loud and clear on your car radio).

Despite the peacefulness you sense today, the region's history is filled with war. Normandy was founded by Viking Norsemen who invaded from the north, settled here in the ninth century, and gave the region its name. A couple of hundred years later, William the Conqueror invaded England from Normandy. His victory is commemorated in a remarkable tapestry at Bayeux. A few hundred years after that, France's greatest cheerleader, Joan of Arc (Jeanne d'Arc), was convicted of heresy in Rouen and burned at the stake by the English, against whom she rallied France during the Hundred Years' War. And in 1944, Normandy was the site of a WWII battle that changed the course of history.

The rugged, rainy coast of Normandy harbors wartime bunkers and enchanting fishing villages like Honfleur. And, on the border it shares with Brittany, the almost surreal island abbey of Mont St-Michel rises serene and majestic, oblivious to the tides of tourists.

PLANNING YOUR TIME

Honfleur, the D-Day beaches, and Mont St-Michel each merit overnight visits. At a minimum, you'll want a full day for the D-Day beaches and a half-day each in Honfleur and on Mont St-Michel. For many, Normandy makes the perfect jet-lag antidote;

Rouen, which is quick to reach by car or train from either Paris or Beauvais airports, makes a good first stop for your trip.

If you're driving between Paris and Honfleur, Giverny or Rouen are easy to visit. By train, they're best as day trips from Paris. The WWII memorial museum in Caen works well as a stop between Honfleur and Bayeux (and the D-Day beaches). Mont St-Michel must be seen early or late to avoid the masses of midday tourists. Dinan, just 45 minutes by car from Mont St-Michel, offers a fine introduction to Brittany. Drivers can enjoy Mont St-Michel as a day trip from Dinan.

For practical information in English about Normandy, see www.normandy.angloinfo.com or www.normandie-tourisme.fr.

GETTING AROUND NORMANDY

This region is ideal with a **car**. If you're driving into Honfleur from the north, take the impressive but pricey Normandy Bridge (Pont de Normandie, €5.40 toll). If you're driving from Mont St-Michel into Brittany, follow my recommended scenic route to the town of St-Malo.

Trains from Paris serve Rouen, Caen, Bayeux, Mont St-Michel (via Pontorson or Rennes), and Dinan, though service between these sights can be frustrating (try linking by bus—see below). Mont St-Michel is a headache by train, except from Paris. Enterprising businesses in Bayeux run a shuttle service between Bayeux and Mont St-Michel—a great help to those without cars.

Buses make Giverny, Honfleur, Arromanches, and Mont St-Michel accessible to train stations in nearby towns, though Sundays offer less frequent connections. Plan ahead: For bus information in English, check with the local TI. Or, if you can navigate a bit in French, try the websites for Bus Verts (for Le Havre, Honfleur, Bayeux, Arromanches, and Caen, www.busverts.fr), Keolis (for Mont St-Michel, www.destination-mor… Tibus or Illenoo (for Dinan and St-Malo… illenoo-services.fr). When navigating the… look for are *Horaires* or *Fiches Horaires* (sc… route). Bus companies commonly offer good value and multiride discounts—for example, Bus Verts offers a 20 percent discount if you buy just four tickets (even if you share them with another person).

Another good option is to use an **excursion tour** to link destinations. **Westcapades** provides trips to Mont St-Michel from Dinan and St-Malo, and **Afoot in France** leads quality tours for small groups or individuals.

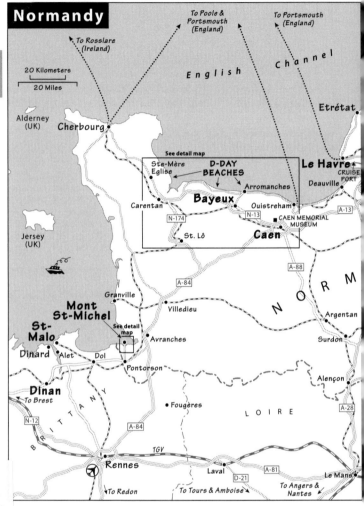

NORMANDY'S CUISINE SCENE

Normandy is known as the land of the four C's: Calvados, Camembert, cider, and *crème*. The region specializes in cream sauces, organ meats (sweetbreads, tripe, and kidneys—the gizzard salads are great), and seafood *(fruits de mer)*. You'll see *crêperies* offering inexpensive and good-value meals everywhere. A *galette* is a savory buckwheat crêpe enjoyed as a main course; a crêpe is sweet and eaten for dessert.

Dairy products are big, too. Local cheeses are Camembert (mild to very strong; see sidebar), Brillat-Savarin (buttery), Liva-

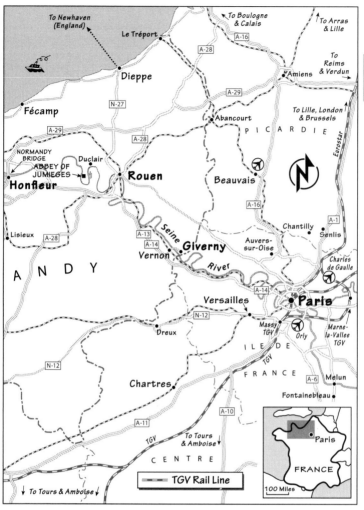

rot (spicy and pungent), Pavé d'Auge (spicy and tangy), and Pont l'Evêque (earthy flavor).

What, no local wine? *Oui*, that's right. Here's how to cope. Fresh, white Muscadet wines are made nearby (in western Loire); they're cheap and a good match with much of Normandy's cuisine. But Normandy is famous for its many apple-based beverages. You can't miss the powerful Calvados apple brandy or the Bénédictine brandy (made by local monks). The local dessert, *trou Normand*, is apple sorbet swimming in Calvados. The region also produces three kinds of alcoholic apple ciders: *Cidre* can be *doux* (sweet), *brut* (dry), or *bouché* (sparkling—and the strongest). You'll also find bottles of Pommeau, a tasty blend of apple juice and Calvados (sold in many

NORMANDY

Camembert Cheese

This cheap, soft, white, Brie-like cheese is sold all over France (and America) in distinctive, round wooden containers. Camembert has been known for its cheese for 500 years, but local legend has it that today's cheese got its start in the French Revolution, when a priest on the run was taken in by Marie Harel, a Camembert farmer. He repaid the favor by giving her the secret formula from his own hometown—Brie.

From cow to customer, Camembert takes about three weeks to make. High-fat milk from Norman cows is curdled with rennet, ladled into round, five-inch molds, sprinkled with *Penicillium camemberti* bacteria, and left to dry. In the first three days, the cheese goes from the cow's body temperature to room temperature to refrigerator cool (50 degrees).

Two weeks later, the ripened and aged cheese is wrapped in wooden bands and labeled for market. Like wines, Camembert cheese is controlled by government regulations and must bear the "A.O.C." *(Appellation d'Origine Contrôlée)* stamp of approval.

shops), as well as *poiré*, a tasty pear cider. And don't leave Normandy without sampling a *kir Normand*, a mix of crème de cassis and cider. Drivers in Normandy should be on the lookout for *Route du Cidre* signs (with a bright red apple); this tourist trail leads you to small producers of handcrafted cider and brandy.

Remember, restaurants serve only during lunch (11:30-14:00) and dinner (19:00-21:00, later in bigger cities); cafés serve food throughout the day.

Rouen

This 2,000-year-old city mixes Gothic architecture, half-timbered houses, and contemporary bustle like no other place in France. Busy Rouen (roo-ahn) is France's fifth-largest port and Europe's biggest food exporter (mostly wheat and grain). Its cobbled old town is a delight to wander, though the city is pretty quiet at night.

Rouen was a regional capital during Roman times, and France's second-largest city in medieval times (with 40,000 residents—only Paris had more). In the ninth century, the Normans made the town their capital.

William the Conqueror called it home before moving to England. Rouen walked a political tightrope between England and France for centuries and was an English base during the Hundred Years' War. Joan of Arc was burned here (in 1431).

Rouen's historic wealth was built on its wool industry and trade—for centuries, it was the last bridge across the Seine River before the Atlantic. In April 1944, as America and Britain weakened German control of Normandy prior to the D-Day landings, Allied bombers destroyed 50 percent of Rouen. And though the industrial suburbs were devastated, most of the historic core survived, keeping Rouen a pedestrian haven.

PLANNING YOUR TIME

If you want a dose of a smaller—yet lively—French city, Rouen is an easy day trip from Paris, with convenient train connections to Gare St. Lazare (nearly hourly, 1.5 hours).

Considering the convenient Paris connection and Rouen's handy location in Normandy, drivers can save headaches by taking the train to Rouen and picking up a rental car there (spend a quiet night in Rouen and pick up your car the next morning). Those already in Paris can take an early train to Rouen, pick up a car, stash your bags in it, leave it in the secure rental lot at the train station, and visit Rouen before heading out to explore Normandy (for car-rental companies, see "Helpful Hints," later).

Even if you don't have a car, you can visit Rouen on your way from Paris to other Normandy destinations, thanks to the good bus and train service (free daytime bag check available at the Museum of Fine Arts, closed Tue).

Orientation to Rouen

Although Paris embraces the Seine, Rouen ignores it. The area we're most interested in is bounded by the river to the south, the Museum of Fine Arts (Esplanade Marcel Duchamp) to the north, Rue de la République to the east, and Place du Vieux Marché to the west. It's a 20-minute walk from the train station to the Notre-Dame Cathedral, and everything else of interest is within a 10-minute walk of the cathedral.

TOURIST INFORMATION

The TI faces the cathedral. Pick up the English map with information on Rouen's museums. The TI also has €5 audioguide tours covering the cathedral and Rouen's historic center, though this book's self-guided walk is enough for most. Ask about sound-and-light shows at the cathedral (generally mid-June-late Sept), and get information about the Route of the Ancient Abbeys if driving (May-Sept Mon-Sat 9:00-19:00, Sun 9:30-12:30 & 14:00-18:00; Oct-April Mon-Sat 9:30-12:30 & 13:30-18:00, closed Sun; free Wi-Fi, 25 Place de la Cathédrale, tel. 02 32 08 32 40, www.rouentourisme.com).

ARRIVAL IN ROUEN

By Train: Rue Jeanne d'Arc cuts straight down from Rouen's train station through the town center to the Seine River. Day-trippers can **walk** from the station down Rue Jeanne d'Arc toward Rue du Gros Horloge—a busy pedestrian mall in the medieval center (and near the starting point of my self-guided walk). While the station has no baggage storage, you can check bags at the Museum of Fine Arts for free during open hours (10-minute downhill walk from the station).

Rouen's **subway** (Métrobus) whisks travelers from under the train station to the Palais de Justice in one stop (€1.60 for 1 hour; buy tickets from machines one level underground, then validate ticket on subway two levels down; subway direction: Technopôle or Georges Braque). Returning to the station, take a subway in direction: Boulingrin and get off at Gare-Rue Verte.

Taxis (to the right as you exit station) will take you to any of my recommended hotels for about €8.

By Car: Finding the city center from the autoroute is tricky—assume you'll get lost for a while. Follow signs for *Centre-Ville* and *Rive Droite* (right bank). You should see signs for *P&R Relais*. These are tram stops outside the center where you can park for free, then hop on a tram (€1.60 each way), avoiding traffic. In the city, you can park in street spaces (metered 8:00-19:00, free overnight), or pay for more secure parking in one of many well-signed underground lots (€5/3 hours. €13/day). For day-trippers taking my self-guided walk of Rouen, the garage under Place du Vieux Marché is best. Other lots are scattered about the city center, and any central spot works. La Haute Vieille Tour parking garage, between the cathedral and the river, is handy for overnighters. When you get turned around (likely, because of the narrow, one-way streets), aim toward the highest cathedral spires you spot.

When leaving Rouen, head for the riverfront road, where autoroute signs will guide you to Paris or to Le Havre and Caen (for D-Day beaches and Honfleur).

HELPFUL HINTS

Closed Days: Most of Rouen's museums are closed on Tuesday, and many sights also close midday (12:00-14:00). The cathedral doesn't open until 14:00 on Monday and is closed during Mass (usually Tue-Sat at 10:00, July-Aug also at 18:00;

Sun and holidays at 8:30, 10:00, and 12:00). The Joan of Arc Church is closed Friday and Sunday mornings, and during Mass.

Market Days: The best open-air market is on Place St. Marc, a few blocks east of St. Maclou Church. It's filled with antiques and other good stuff (all day Tue, Fri, and Sat; on Sun until about 13:30). A smaller market is on Place du Vieux Marché, near the Joan of Arc Church (Tue-Sun until 13:30, closed Mon). The TI has a list of all weekly markets.

Supermarket: Small grocery shops are scattered about the city, and a big **Monoprix** is on Rue du Gros Horloge (groceries at the back, Mon-Sat 8:30-21:00, Sun 9:00-13:00).

Internet Access: The TI has free Wi-Fi. Several cafés with Wi-Fi are within a few blocks of the train station on Rue Jeanne d'Arc.

English Bookstore: ABC Bookshop has nothing but English-language books—some American, but mostly British (Tue-Sat 10:00-18:00, closed Sun-Mon, just south of St. Ouen Church at 11 Rue des Faulx, tel. 02 35 71 08 67).

Taxi: Call **Les Taxi Blancs** at 02 35 61 20 50.

Car Rental: Agencies with an office in the train station include **Europcar** (tel. 02 35 88 21 20), **Avis** (tel. 02 35 88 60 94), and **Hertz** (tel. 02 35 70 70 71).

SNCF Boutique: For train tickets, visit the SNCF office at the corner of Rue aux Juifs and Rue Eugène Boudin (Mon 12:30-19:00, Tue-Sat 10:00-19:00, closed Sun).

Rouen Walk

On this 1.5-hour self-guided walk, you'll see the essential Rouen sights and experience its pedestrian-friendly streets. Remember that many sights are closed midday (12:00-14:00). This walk is designed for day-trippers coming by train, but works just as well for drivers, who should ideally park at or near Place du Vieux Marché (parking garage available), where the walk begins. We'll stroll the length of Rue du Gros Horloge to Notre-Dame Cathedral, visit the plague cemetery (Aître St. Maclou), loop up to the church of St. Ouen, and return along Rue de l'Hôpital. The walk ends at the Museum of Fine Arts, a short walk back to the train station.

• *If arriving by train, walk down Rue Jeanne d'Arc and turn right on Rue du Guillaume le Conquérant (notice the Gothic Palace of Justice building across Rue Jeanne d'Arc—we'll get to that later). This takes you to the back door of our starting point...*

NORMANDY

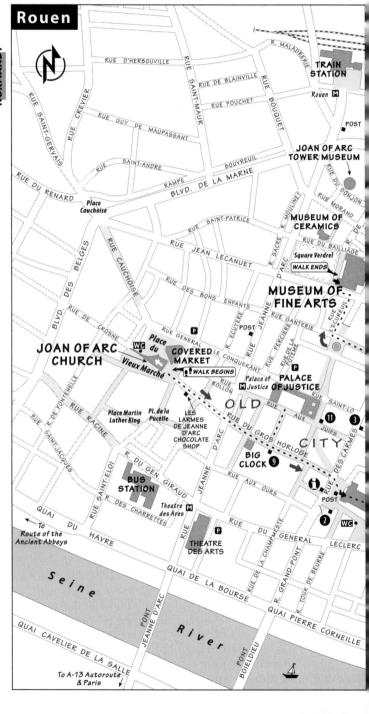

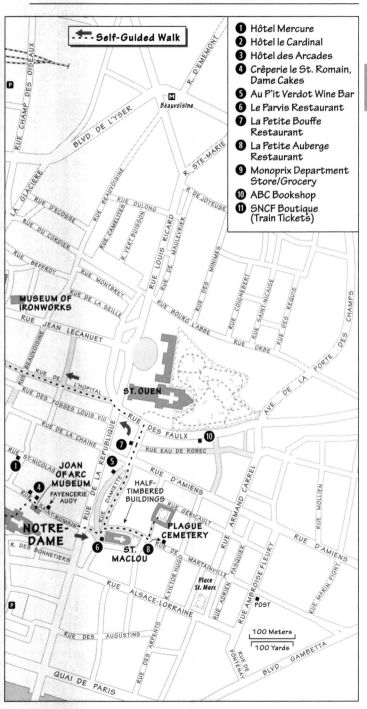

-·-·- Self-Guided Walk

1 Hôtel Mercure
2 Hôtel le Cardinal
3 Hôtel des Arcades
4 Crêperie le St. Romain,
   Dame Cakes
5 Au P'it Verdot Wine Bar
6 Le Parvis Restaurant
7 La Petite Bouffe
   Restaurant
8 La Petite Auberge
   Restaurant
9 Monoprix Department
   Store/Grocery
10 ABC Bookshop
11 SNCF Boutique
   (Train Tickets)

NORMANDY

The Hundred Years' War (1336-1453)

It would take a hundred years to explain all the causes, battles, and political maneuverings of this century-plus of warfare between France and England, but here goes:

In 1300, before the era of the modern nation-state, the borders between France and England were fuzzy. French-speaking kings had ruled England, English kings owned the south of France, and English merchants dominated trade in the north. Dukes and lords in both countries were aligned more along family lines than by national identity. When the French king died without a male heir (1328), both France and England claimed the crown, and the battle was on.

England invaded the more populous country (1345) and—thanks to skilled archers using armor-penetrating longbows—won big battles at Crécy (1346) and Poitiers (1356). Despite a truce, roving bands of English mercenaries stayed behind and supported themselves by looting French villages. The French responded with guerrilla tactics.

In 1415, the English took still more territory, with Henry V's big victory at Agincourt. But rallied by the heavenly visions of young Joan of Arc, the French slowly drove the invaders out. Paris was liberated in 1436, and when Bordeaux fell to French forces (1453), the fighting ended without a treaty.

Place du Vieux Marché

Stand in the small garden near the entrance of the striking Joan of Arc Church. Surrounded by half-timbered buildings, this old market square houses a cute, covered produce and fish market, a park commemorating Joan of Arc's burning, and a modern church named after her. Find the towering aluminum cross. This marks the spot where Rouen publicly punished and executed people. The pillories stood here, and during the Revolution, the town's guillotine made 800 people "a foot shorter at the top." In 1431, Joan of Arc—only 19 years old—was burned right here. Find her flaming statue (built into the wall of the church, facing the cross). As the flames engulfed her, an English soldier said, "Oh my God, we've killed a saint." Nearly 500 years later, Joan was canonized, and the soldier was proved right.

• *Now step inside...*

▲Joan of Arc Church (Eglise Jeanne d'Arc)

This modern church is a tribute to the young woman who was canonized in 1920 and later became the patron saint of France. The church, completed in 1979, feels Scandinavian inside and out—another reminder of Normandy's Nordic roots. Sumptuous 16th-century windows, salvaged from a church lost during World War

II, were worked into the soft architectural lines (the €0.50 English pamphlet provides some background and describes the stained-glass scenes). The pointed, stake-like support columns to the right seem fitting for a church dedicated to a woman burned at the stake. Similar to modern churches designed by the 20th-century architect Le Corbusier, this is an uplifting place to be, with a ship's-hull vaulting and sweeping wood ceiling that sail over curved pews and a wall of glass below. Make time to savor this unusual sanctuary.

Cost and Hours: Free, Mon-Thu and Sat 10:00-12:00 & 14:00-18:00, Fri 10:00-12:00, Sun 14:00-17:30, closed during Mass. A public WC is 30 yards straight ahead from the church doors.

• *Turn left out of the church and step over the ruins of a 15th-century church that once stood on this spot (destroyed during the French Revolution). Leave the square and join the busy pedestrian street, Rue du Gros Horloge—the town's main shopping street since Roman times. A block up on your right (at #163) is Rouen's most famous chocolate shop...*

Auzou

At Auzou, the makers of Les Larmes de Jeanne d'Arc would love to tempt you with their chocolate-covered almond "tears *(larmes)* of Joan of Arc." Although you must resist touching the chocolate fountain, you are welcome to taste a tear (delicious). The first one is free; a small bag costs about €9 (Mon 14:00-19:15, Tue-Sat 9:15-19:15, Sun 9:15-12:45).

• *Your route continues past a medieval McDonald's and across busy Rue Jeanne d'Arc to the...*

▲Big Clock (Gros Horloge)

This impressive, circa-1528 Renaissance clock, le Gros Horloge (groh or-lohzh), decorates the former City Hall. Originally, the clock had only an hour hand (it's now under restoration) but no minute hand. In the 16th century, an hour hand offered sufficient precision; minute hands became necessary only in a later, faster-paced age. The silver orb above the clock makes one revolution in 29 days. The town medallion (sculpted into the stone below the clock) features a sacrificial lamb, which has both religious meaning (Jesus is the Lamb of God) and commercial significance (wool was the source of Rouen's wealth). The clock's artistic highlight fills the underside of the arch (walk underneath and stretch your back), with the "Good Shepherd" and loads of sheep.

Bell Tower Panorama: To see the inner workings of the clock and an extraordinary panorama over Rouen (including a stirring view of the cathedral), climb the clock tower's 100 steps. You'll tour several rooms with the help of a friendly, 40-minute audioguide and learn about life in Rouen when the tower was built. The big

NORMANDY

bells at the top weigh 1 to 2 tons each and ring on the hour—a deafening experience if you're in the tower. Don't miss the 360-degree view outside from the very top (€6, includes audioguide; Tue-Sun 10:00-13:00 & 14:00-19:00, 14:00-18:00 only Nov-March, closed Mon year-round, last entry one hour before closing).

• *Walk under le Gros Horloge and continue straight a half-block, then take a one-block detour left (up Rue Thouret) to see the...*

Palace of Justice (Palais de Justice)

Years of cleaning have removed the grime that once covered this fabulously flamboyant Gothic building, the former home of Normandy's *parlement* and the largest civil Gothic building in France. The result is striking; think of this as you visit Rouen's other Gothic structures—some are awaiting baths of their own. Pockmarks on the side of the building that faces Rue Jeanne d'Arc are leftovers from bombings during the Normandy invasion. Look for the English-language plaques on the iron fence—they provide some history and describe the damage and tedious repair process.

• *Double back and continue up Rue du Gros Horloge. In a block you'll see a stone plaque dedicated to **Cavelier de la Salle** (high on the left), who explored the mouth of the Mississippi River, claimed the state of Louisiana for France, and was assassinated in Texas in 1687. Soon you'll reach...*

▲▲Notre-Dame Cathedral (Cathédrale Notre-Dame)

This cathedral is a landmark of art history. You're seeing essentially what Claude Monet saw as he painted 30 different studies of this

frilly Gothic facade at various times of the day. Using the physical building only as a rack upon which to hang light, mist, dusk, and shadows, Monet was capturing "impressions." One of the results is in Rouen's Museum of Fine Arts; four others are at the Orsay Museum in Paris. Find the plaque showing one of these paintings (in the corner of the square, about 30 paces to your right if you were exiting the TI).

Cost and Hours: Free, Tue-Sun 8:00-19:00 except Nov-March closed for lunch 12:00-14:00; Mon 14:00-19:00; closed during Mass—Tue-Sat at 10:00, July-Aug also at 18:00, Sun and holidays at 8:30, 10:30, and 12:00.

Cathedral Exterior: There's been a church on this site for more than a thousand years. Charlemagne honored it with a visit in the eighth century before the Vikings sacked it a hundred years later. The building you see today was constructed between the 12th and 14th centuries, though lightning strikes, wars (the cathedral was devastated in WWII fighting), and other destructive forces meant constant rebuilding—which explains the difference in the towers, such as the stones used at each tower's base.

Look up at the elaborate, soaring facade and find the cleaned sections, with bright statues on either side of the central portal—later, we'll meet some of their friends face-to-face inside the cathedral. The facade is another fine Rouen example of Flamboyant Gothic, and the spire, soaring nearly 500 feet high, is awe-inspiring. Why such a big cathedral here? Until the 1700s, Rouen was the second-largest city in France—rich from its wool trade and its booming port. On summer evenings, there may be a colorful sound-and-light show at the cathedral's facade (ask at the TI, starts at dark, which means about 23:00 in June and July).

Above the main door is a marvelous depiction of the Tree of Jesse. Jesse, King David's father, is shown reclined, resting his head on his hand, looking nonplussed. The tree grows from Jesse's back; the figures that sprout from its branches represent the lineage of Jesus. Compare this happy scene with the many Last Judgments you have seen decorating other church portals.

Cathedral Interior: Look down the center of the **nave.** This is a classic Gothic nave—four stories of pointed-arch arcades, the top filled with windows to help light the interior. Today, the interior is lighter than intended because the original colored glass (destroyed mostly in World War II) was replaced by clear glass.

Circle counterclockwise around the church, starting down the right aisle. The side chapels and windows have brief descriptions in English, each dedicated to a different saint. These chapels display the changing assortment of styles through the centuries. Look for photos halfway down on the right that show WWII bomb damage to the cathedral.

Passing through an iron gate after the high altar (closed during Mass; may be open on the opposite side even during Mass), you come to several **stone statues.** These figures were lifted from the facade during a cleaning and should eventually be installed in a museum. For us, it's a rare chance to stand toe-to-toe with a saint (weird feeling).

There are several **stone tombs** on your left, dating from when Rouen was the Norman capital. The first tomb is for Rollo, the first duke of Normandy in 933 (and great-great-great-great grandfather of William the Conqueror, seventh duke of Normandy, c. 1028). As the first duke, Rollo was chief of the first gang of Vikings (the original "Normans") who decided to settle here. Called the "Father of Normandy," Rollo died at the age of 80, but he is portrayed on his tomb as if he were 33 (as was the fashion, because Jesus died at that age). Because of later pillage and plunder, only Rollo's femur is inside the tomb.

And speaking of body parts, the next tomb contains the heart of Richard the Lionhearted. (The rest of his body lies in the Abbey of Fontevraud.)

Circle behind the altar. The beautiful **windows** with bold blues and reds are generally from the 13th century. Look back above the entry to see a rare black-and-white rose window (its medieval colored glass is long gone). You'll come to a display for the window dedicated to St. Julien, with pane-by-pane descriptions in English.

Continue a few paces, then look up to the **ceiling** over the nave. Looking directly above Rollo's femur on the opposite side of the apse, you can see the patchwork in the ceiling where the spire crashed through the roof. Perhaps this might be a good time to exit? Pass through the small iron gate, turn right, and leave through the side door (north transept). (If the door is closed, head back out through the main entrance, turn right, then loop back alongside the church.)

Stepping outside, look back at the **facade** over the door. The fine carved tympanum (the area over the door) shows a graphic Last Judgment. Jesus stands between the saved (on the left) and the damned (on the right). Notice the devil grasping a miser, who clutches a bag of coins. On the far right, look for the hellish hot tub, where even a bishop (pointy hat) is eternally in hot water. And is it my imagination, or are those saved souls on the far left high-fiving each other?

Most of the facade has been cleaned—blasted with jets of water—but the limestone carving is still black. It's too delicate to survive the hosing. A more expensive laser cleaning has begun, and the result is astonishing.

From this courtyard, a gate deposits you on a traffic-free street. Turn right and walk along the appealing Rue St. Romain. In a short distance, you can look up through an opening above the entrance to the Joan of Arc Museum (described next) and gaze back at the cathedral's prickly **spire.** Made of cast iron in the late 1800s—about the same time Gustave Eiffel was building his tower in Paris—the spire is, at 490 feet, the tallest in France. You can also see the former location of the missing smaller (green) spire—downed in a violent 1999 storm that blew the spire off the roof and sent it crashing to the cathedral floor.

• *To learn more about Rouen's most famous figure, consider touring the...*

▲▲Joan of Arc Museum (Historial Jeanne d'Arc)

In 2015, Rouen finally got the in-depth, state-of-the-art Joan of Arc museum it deserves, housed in what was once the archbishop's

Joan of Arc (1412-1431)

The cross-dressing teenager who rallied French soldiers to drive out English invaders was the illiterate daughter of a humble farmer. One summer day, in her dad's garden, 13-year-old Joan heard a heavenly voice accompanied by bright light. It was the first of several saints (including Michael, Margaret, and Catherine) to talk to her during her short life.

In 1429, the young girl was instructed by the voices to save France from the English. Dressed in men's clothing, she traveled to see the king and predicted that the French armies would be defeated near Orléans—as they were. King Charles VII equipped her with an ancient sword and a banner that read "Jesus, Maria," and sent her to rally the troops.

Soon "the Maid" (la Pucelle) was bivouacking amid rough soldiers, riding with them into battle, and suffering an arrow wound to the chest—all while liberating the town of Orléans. On July 17, 1429, she held her banner high in the cathedral of Reims as Charles was officially proclaimed king of a resurgent France.

Joan and company next tried to retake Paris (1429), but the English held out. She suffered a crossbow wound through the thigh, and her reputation of invincibility was tarnished. During a battle at Compiègne (1430), she was captured and turned over to the English for £10,000. The English took her to Rouen, where she was chained by the neck inside an iron cage while the local French authorities (allied with the English) plotted against her. The Inquisition—insisting that Joan's voices were "false and diabolical"—tried and sentenced her to death for being a witch and a heretic.

On May 30, 1431, Joan of Arc was tied to a stake on Rouen's old market square (Place du Vieux Marché). She yelled, "Rouen! Rouen! Must I die here?" Then they lit the fire; she fixed her eyes on a crucifix and died chanting, "Jesus, Jesus, Jesus."

After her death, Joan's place in history was slowly rehabilitated. French authorities proclaimed her trial illegal (1455), and she quickly became the most important symbol of French nationhood. Over the centuries, prominent writers and artists were inspired by her, politicians co-opted her fame for their own purposes, and common people rallied around her idealized image. Finally, the Catholic Church beatified (1909) and canonized her (1920) as St. Joan of Arc.

palace—where Joan of Arc was tried and sentenced to death. A 1.25-hour multimedia experience (translated to English in your headphones) brings you to her rehabilitation trial, 20 years after her execution, where eyewitnesses describe key events. A docent leads you from room to room as you twist up through the tower, ending with the grand finale in l'Officialité—the room where the trial actually took place. You're then set free to explore exhibits examining the role Joan of Arc has played in French culture over the centuries. The complete experience is entertaining and informative.

Cost and Hours: €9.50, Tue-Sun 9:45-19:45, until 20:45 Fri-Sat in summer, closed Mon year-round, last entry 1.75 hours before closing, 7 Rue St. Romain, tel. 02 35 52 48 00, www.historial-jeannedarc.fr.

• *From the museum, continue down atmospheric Rue St. Romain. A bit farther down the street at #26, find the shop marked...*

Fayencerie Augy

Monsieur Augy and his staff welcome shoppers to browse his studio/gallery/shop and see Rouen's clay "china" being made the traditional way. First, the clay is molded and fired. Then it's dipped in white enamel, dried, lovingly hand painted, and fired a second time. Rouen was the first city in France to make faience, earthenware with colored glazes. In the 1700s, the town had 18 factories churning out the popular product (Mon-Sat 9:00-19:00, closed Sun, 26 Rue St. Romain, VAT tax refunds nearly pay for the shipping, www.fayencerie-augy.com). For more faience, visit the local Museum of Ceramics (described later, under "Sights in Rouen").

• *Continue along Rue St. Romain, which (after crossing Rue de la République) leads to the fancy...*

St. Maclou Church

This church's unique, bowed facade is textbook Flamboyant Gothic. Its recent cleaning revealed a brilliant white stone. Notice the flame-like tracery decorating its gable. Because this was built at the very end of the Gothic age—and construction took many years—the doors are from the next age: the Renaissance (c. 1550). Study the graphic Last Judgment above the doors; it was designed when Rouen was riddled with the Black Plague. The bright and airy interior is worth a quick peek.

Cost and Hours: Free, Sat-Mon 10:00-12:00 & 14:00-18:00, closed Tue-Fri.

• *Leaving the church, turn right, and then take another right (giving the little boys on the corner wall a wide berth). Wander past a fine wall of half-timbered buildings fronting Rue Martainville, to the end of St. Maclou Church.*

Half-Timbered Buildings

Because the local stone—a chalky limestone from the cliffs of the Seine River—was of poor quality (your thumbnail is stronger), and because local oak was plentiful, half-timbered buildings became a Rouen specialty from the 14th through 19th century. Cantilevered floors were standard until the early 1500s. These top-heavy designs made sense: City land was limited, property taxes were based on ground-floor square footage, and the cantilevering minimized unsupported spans on upper floors. The oak beams provided the structural skeleton of the building, which was then filled in with a mix of clay, straw, pebbles, or whatever was available.

NORMANDY

• *About 50 yards past the end of the church, on the left at 186 Rue Martainville, a covered lane leads to the...*

▲Plague Cemetery (Aître St. Maclou)

During the great plagues of the Middle Ages, as many as two-thirds of the people in this parish died. For the decimated community, dealing with the corpses was an overwhelming task. This half-timbered courtyard (c. 1520) was a mass grave, an ossuary where the bodies were "processed." Bodies would be dumped into the grave (where the well is now) and drenched in liquid lime to help speed decomposition. Later, the bones would be stacked in alcoves above the colonnades that line this courtyard. Notice the ghoulish carvings (c. 1560s) of gravediggers' tools, skulls, crossbones, and characters doing the "dance of death." In this *danse macabre*, Death, the great equalizer, grabs people of all social classes. The place is now an art school. Peek in on the young artists. As you leave, spy the dried black cat (died c. 1520, in tiny glass case to the left of the door). To overcome evil, it was buried during the building's construction.

Cost and Hours: Free, daily 9:00-18:00.

Nearby: Farther down Rue Martainville, at Place St. Marc, a colorful market blooms Sunday until about 13:30 and all day Tuesday, Friday, and Saturday. If it's not market day, you can double back to the cathedral and Rue du Gros Horloge, or continue with me to explore more of Rouen and find the Museum of Fine Arts (back toward the train station).

• *To reach the museum, turn right upon leaving the boneyard, then right again at the little boys (onto Rue Damiette), and hike up antique row to the vertical St. Ouen Church (a seventh-century abbey turned church in the 15th century, fine park behind). Turn left at the church on Rue des Faulx (the ABC Bookshop is two blocks to the right—see "Helpful Hints," earlier) and cross the busy street (the horseman you see to the right is a short-yet-majestic Napoleon Bonaparte who welcomes visitors to Rouen's city hall).*

*Continue down Rue de l'Hôpital's traffic-free lane, which becomes Rue Ganterie (admire the Gothic fountain at Rue Beauvoisine). A right at the modern square on Rue de l'Ecureuil leads you to the **Museum of Fine Arts** and the **Museum of Ironworks** (both described next, under "Sights in Rouen"). This is the end of our tour. The tower where Joan of Arc was imprisoned (also explained later) is a few blocks uphill, on the way back to the train station.*

NORMANDY

Sights in Rouen

The first three museums are within a block of one another, closed on Tuesdays, never crowded, and can all be visited with the same combo-ticket (www.rouen-musees.com).

▲Museum of Fine Arts (Musée des Beaux-Arts)

Paintings from many periods are beautifully displayed in this overlooked two-floor museum, including works by Caravaggio, Peter Paul Rubens, Paolo Veronese, Jan Steen, Velázquez, Théodore Géricault, Jean-Auguste-Dominique Ingres, Eugène Delacroix, and several Impressionists. With its reasonable entry fee and calm interior, this museum is worth a short visit for the Impressionists and a surgical hit of a few other key artists. The museum café is good for a peaceful break.

Cost and Hours: €5, €8 combo-ticket includes ironworks and ceramics museums; Wed-Mon 10:00-18:00, closed Tue; a few blocks below train station at 26 bis Rue Jean Lecanuet, tel. 02 35 71 28 40.

Visiting the Museum: Pick up the essential museum map at the info desk as you enter. Consider a stop in the meditative café to plan your attack.

Climb the grand staircase to the second floor, where you'll focus your time and savor the lack of crowds. Find the excellent handheld English descriptions in key rooms. The museum is divided into two wings on either side of the main stairway. Turning right when you reach the second floor, you'll pass through a few rooms, then start seeing some names you recognize: Ingres and Jacques-Louis David (Room 2.21) and then a good collection of works by Géricault (Room 2.22). Turn left into Room 2.33, with one of Monet's famous paintings of the Rouen cathedral facade. Now loop through this wing to enjoy scenes inspired by Normandy's landscape and works by Impressionist greats; the lineup here often includes Monet, Sisley, Pissarro, Renoir, Degas, and Corot. Take a moment to also appreciate beautiful paintings by Impressionists whose names you may not recognize. Room 2.25 showcases a scene of Rouen's busy port in 1855.

Paintings on the other side of the second floor are devoted to French painters from the 17th and 18th centuries (Boucher, Fragonard, and Poussin) and Italian works, including several by Veronese. A gripping Caravaggio canvas (Room 2.4), depicting the flagellation of Christ, demands attention with its dramatic lighting and realistic faces.

Stairs at the rear, near the Caravaggio, lead down to an intriguing collection of works by 16th-century Dutch and Belgian artists and a small room of medieval icons. On the other side of the first floor, pass through the bookstore to find a collection of paintings by hometown boy Raymond Duchamp-Villon (brother of the famous Dadaist Marcel Duchamp), several colorful Modiglianis, and one grand-scale Delacroix.

Museum of Ironworks (Musée le Secq des Tournelles, a.k.a. Musée de la Ferronnerie)

This deconsecrated church houses iron objects, many of them more than 1,500 years old. Locks, chests, keys, tools, thimbles, coffee grinders, corkscrews, and flatware from centuries ago—virtually anything made of iron is on display. You can duck into the entry area for a glimpse of a medieval iron scene without passing through the turnstile.

Cost and Hours: €3, €8 combo-ticket includes fine arts and ceramics museums, no English explanations—bring a French/English dictionary, Wed-Mon 14:00-18:00, closed Tue, behind Museum of Fine Arts, 2 Rue Jacques Villon, tel. 02 35 88 42 92.

Museum of Ceramics (Musée de la Céramique)

Rouen's famous faience (earthenware), which dates from the 16th to 18th century, fills this fine old mansion. There's not a word of English except in the museum leaflet.

Cost and Hours: €3, €8 combo-ticket includes fine arts and ironworks museums, same hours as Museum of Ironworks, 1 Rue Faucon, tel. 02 35 07 31 74.

Joan of Arc Tower (La Tour Jeanne d'Arc)

This massive tower (1204), part of Rouen's brooding castle, was Joan's prison before her untimely death. Cross the deep moat and find three small floors (and 122 spiral steps) covering tidbits of Rouen's and Joan's history, well-described in English. The top floor gives a good peek at an impressive wood substructure but no views.

Cost and Hours: €2, Wed-Sat and Mon 10:00-12:30 & 14:00-18:00, Sun 14:00-18:30, closed Tue, one block uphill from the Museum of Fine Arts on Rue du Bouvreuil, tel. 02 35 98 16 21.

NEAR ROUEN
The Route of the Ancient Abbeys
(La Route des Anciennes Abbayes)

This route—punctuated with medieval abbeys, apples, cherry trees, and Seine River views—provides a pleasing detour for drivers connecting Rouen and Honfleur or the D-Day beaches (if you're traveling *sans* car, skip it). The only "essential" stop on this drive is the Abbey of Jumièges.

From Rouen, follow the Seine along its right bank and track signs for D-982 to Duclair, then follow D-65 to Jumièges. From near Jumièges you can cross the Seine on the tiny, free-and-frequent car ferry, then connect with the A-13, or continue following the right bank of the Seine and cross at the Pont de Tancarville bridge (free) or the magnificent Normandy Bridge (Pont de Normandie, €5.40). By either route allow 45 minutes from Rouen to Jumièges and another 75 minutes to Honfleur, or two more hours to Bayeux.

Fifteen minutes west of Rouen, drivers can stop to admire the gleaming Romanesque church at the **Abbey of St. Georges de Boscherville** (skip the abbey grounds). This perfectly intact and beautiful church makes for interesting comparisons with the ruined church at Jumièges. The café across from the church is good for meals or drinks.

Farther along the route is the **Abbey of Jumièges,** a spiritual place for lovers of evocative ruins (worth ▲). Founded in A.D. 654 as a Benedictine abbey, it was leveled by Vikings in the ninth century, then rebuilt by William the Conqueror in the 11th century. This magnificent complex thrived for centuries as Normandy's largest abbey. It was part of a great monastic movement that reestablished civilization in Normandy out of the chaos that followed the fall of Rome. The abbey was destroyed during the French Revolution, when it was used as a quarry. The abbey has changed little since then. Today there is no roof to protect the abbey, and many walls are entirely gone. But what remains of the abbey's Church of Notre-Dame is awe-inspiring. Study its stark Romanesque facade standing 160 feet high. Stroll down the nave's center; notice the three levels of arches and the soaring rear wall capped by a lantern tower to light the choir. Find a seat in the ruined choir and imagine the church before its destruction. You'll discover brilliant views of the ruins and better appreciate its importance by wandering into the park (€6.50, helpful English handout and explanations posted, more detailed booklet for sale, daily mid-April-mid-Sept 9:30-18:30, mid-Sept-mid-April 9:30-13:00 & 14:30-17:30, unnecessary videoguide-€5, tel. 02 35 37 24 02, www.abbayedejumieges.fr). Decent lunch options lie across the street from the abbey.

Sleeping in Rouen

Although I prefer Rouen by day, sleeping here presents you with a mostly tourist-free city (most hotels cater to business travelers). These hotels are perfectly central, within two blocks of Notre-Dame Cathedral.

$$$ Hôtel Mercure*,** ideally situated a block north of the cathedral, is a concrete business hotel with a professional staff, a stay-awhile lobby and bar, and 125 small but well-equipped and

NORMANDY

Sleep Code

Abbreviations   (€1=$1.10, country code: 33)
S=Single, **D**=Double/Twin, **T**=Triple, **Q**=Quad, **b**=bathroom,
*=French hotel rating (0-5 stars)
Price Rankings
  $$$ **Higher Priced**—Most rooms €95 or more
   $$ **Moderately Priced**—Most rooms €60-95
    $ **Lower Priced**—Most rooms €60 or less
Unless otherwise noted, credit cards are accepted, breakfast
is not included, free Wi-Fi and/or a guest computer is gener-
ally available, and English is spoken. Prices change; verify cur-
rent rates online or by email. For the best prices, always book
directly with the hotel.

---

modern rooms. Suites come with views of the cathedral, but are
pricey and not much bigger than a double. Look for big discounts
online (standard Db-€125, "privilege" Db-€30 extra, suite-€50
extra, breakfast-€18, air-con, elevator, parking garage-€14/day, 7
Rue Croix de Fer, tel. 02 35 52 69 52, www.mercure.com, h1301@
accor.com).

$$$ Hôtel le Cardinal** is a solid value with 15 sharp, well-
designed rooms, most with point-blank views of the cathedral and
all with queen-size beds and modern bathrooms (standard Db-
€88-120; €145-185 for fourth-floor rooms—the hotel's largest,
with balconies and great cathedral views; nonsmoking rooms avail-
able, breakfast-€9, elevator, 1 Place de la Cathédrale, tel. 02 35 70
24 42, www.cardinal-hotel.fr, hotelcardinal.rouen@wanadoo.fr).

$ Hôtel des Arcades is bare-bones basic, but as cheap and cen-
tral as it gets (S-€47, S with shower only-€55, Sb-€60, D-€52, D
with shower only-€60, Db-€65, breakfast-€6, 52 Rue des Carmes,
tel. 02 35 70 10 30, www.hotel-des-arcades.fr, hotel_des_arcades@
yahoo.fr).

Eating in Rouen

You can eat well in Rouen at fair prices. Because you're in Norman-
dy, *crêperies* abound. To find the best eating action, prowl the streets
between the St. Maclou and St. Ouen churches (Rues Martainville
and Damiette) for *crêperies*, wine bars, international cuisine, and
traditional restaurants. This is Rouen's liveliest area at night, except
for Sunday and Monday, when many places are closed.

Crêperie le St. Romain, between the cathedral and St. Ma-
clou Church, is an excellent budget option. It's run by gentle Mr.
Pegis, who serves filling €10-11 crêpes with small salads and offers
many good options in a warm setting (tables in the rear are best).

The hearty *gatiflette* is delicious (lunch Tue-Sat, dinner Thu-Sat, closed Mon and sometimes Sun, 52 Rue St. Romain, tel. 02 35 88 90 36).

Dame Cakes is ideal if it's lunchtime or teatime and you need a Jane Austen fix. The decor is from a more precious era, and the baked goods are out of this world. Locals adore the tables in the back garden, while tourists eat up the cathedral view from the first-floor room (€7 salads, €11 *plats,* available only at lunch, garden terrace in back, Mon-Sat 10:30-19:00, closed Sun, 70 Rue St. Romain, tel. 02 35 07 49 31).

Au P'it Verdot is a lively wine bar-café where locals gather for a glass of wine and appetizers—not big meals, just meat-and-cheese plates—in the thick of restaurant row (closed Sun-Mon, 13 Rue Père Adam, tel. 02 35 36 34 43).

Le Parvis, which faces St. Maclou Church, is a good bet for a Norman meal featuring homemade cuisine. There's comfortable seating inside and out (€25 two-course *menu,* €29 three-course *menu,* ask about their *bouillabaisse à la mode Normande,* closed for dinner Sun and all day Mon, 7 Place Barthlémy, tel. 02 35 15 28 80).

La Petite Bouffe is a young-at-heart, appealing, cheery place with tall windows. It's not high cuisine, but the choices are fun and the prices are very reasonable (€20 three-course *menus,* inside dining only, closed Sun, 1 Rue des Boucheries St-Ouen, tel. 02 35 98 13 14).

La Petite Auberge, a block off Rue Damiette, is the most traditional place I list. It has an Old World interior, reasonable prices, and it's also open on Sunday (*menus* from €23, closed Mon, 164 Rue Martainville, tel. 02 35 70 80 18).

Rouen Connections

Rouen is well served by trains from Paris and Caen, making Bayeux and the D-Day beaches a snap to reach.

From Rouen by Train to: Paris' Gare St. Lazare (nearly hourly, 1.5 hours), **Bayeux** (14/day, 2.5 hours, change in Caen), **Caen** (14/day, 1.5 hours), **Pontorson/Mont St-Michel** (2/day, 4 hours, change in Caen; more with change in Paris, 7 hours).

By Train and Bus to: Honfleur (6/day Mon-Sat, 3/day Sun, 1-hour train to Le Havre, then easy transfer to 30-minute bus over Normandy Bridge to Honfleur—Le Havre's bus and train stations are adjacent).

Honfleur

Gazing at its cozy harbor lined with skinny, soaring houses, it's easy to overlook the historic importance of Honfleur (ohn-flur). For more than a thousand years, sailors have enjoyed this port's ideal location, where the Seine River greets the English Channel. William the Conqueror received supplies shipped from Honfleur. Samuel de Champlain sailed from here in 1608 to North America, where he discovered the St. Lawrence River and founded Quebec City. The town was also a fa-

vorite of 19th-century Impressionists who were captivated by Honfleur's unusual light—the result of its river-meets-sea setting. Eugène Boudin (boo-dahn) lived and painted in Honfleur, drawing Monet and other creative types from Paris. In some ways, modern art was born in the fine light of idyllic little Honfleur.

Honfleur escaped the bombs of World War II, and today offers a romantic port enclosed on three sides by sprawling outdoor cafés. Long eclipsed by the gargantuan port of Le Havre just across the Seine, Honfleur happily uses its past as a bar stool...and sits on it.

Orientation to Honfleur

Honfleur is popular—expect crowds on weekends and during summer. All of Honfleur's appealing lanes and activities are within a short stroll of its old port (Vieux Bassin). The Seine River flows just east of the center, the hills of the Côte de Grâce form its western limit, and Rue de la République slices north-south through the center to the port. Honfleur has two can't-miss sights—the harbor and Ste. Catherine Church—and a handful of other intriguing monuments. But really, the town itself is its best sight.

TOURIST INFORMATION

The TI is in the glassy public library *(Mediathéque)* on Quai le Paulmier, two blocks from the Vieux Bassin toward Le Havre (July-Aug Mon-Sat 9:30-19:00, Sun 10:00-17:00; Sept-June Mon-Sat 9:30-12:30 & 14:00-18:30, Sun 10:00-12:30 & 14:00-17:00 except closed Sun afternoon Oct-Easter; free WCs, pay Wi-Fi, tel. 02 31 89 23 30, www.ot-honfleur.fr). Here you can rent a €3.50 audioguide for a self-guided town walk, or pick up a town map, bus and train schedules, and find information on the D-Day beaches.

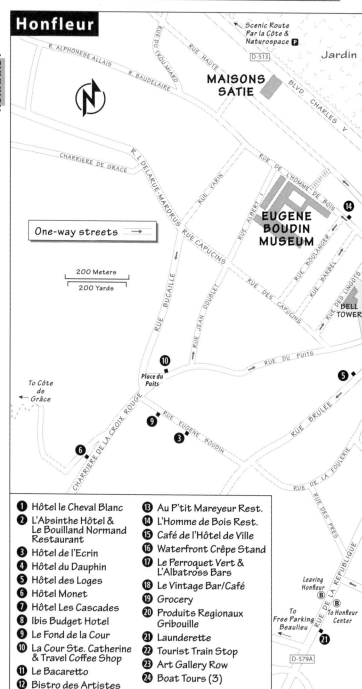

Honfleur

*Scenic Route
Par la Côte &
Naturospace* **P**

Jardin

D-513

**MAISONS
SATIE**

R. ALPHONESE ALLAIS

R. DU TROUILMARD

RUE HAUTE

R. BAUDELAIRE

BLVD. CHARLES V

CHARRIERE DE GRACE

R L DELARUE-MARDRUS

RUE VARIN

RUE DE L'HOMME DE BOIS

One-way streets →

RUE CAPUCINS

RUE ALBERT I

**EUGENE
BOUDIN
MUSEUM**

RUE BOULANGER

❶❹

RUE BARBEL

200 Meters

200 Yards

RUE BUCAILLE

RUE JEAN DOUBLET

RUE DES CAPUCINS

RUE DES LINGOTS

**BELL
TOWER**

RUE DU PUITS

❿
*Place du
Puits*

❺

*To Côte
de
← Grâce*

❾

RUE EUGENE BOUDIN

RUE BRULEE

❻

❸

CHARRIERE DE LA CROIX ROUGE

RUE DE LA TOUERIE

RUE DES PRES

*Leaving
Honfleur*
Ⓑ

*To Honfleur
Center*

RUE DE LA REPUBLIQUE

*To
Free Parking
Beaulieu*

Ⓑ

㉑

D-579A

❶ Hôtel le Cheval Blanc	❸ Au P'tit Mareyeur Rest.
❷ L'Absinthe Hôtel & Le Bouilland Normand Restaurant	❹ L'Homme de Bois Rest.
	❺ Café de l'Hôtel de Ville
❸ Hôtel de l'Ecrin	❻ Waterfront Crêpe Stand
❹ Hôtel du Dauphin	❼ Le Perroquet Vert & L'Albatross Bars
❺ Hôtel des Loges	
❻ Hôtel Monet	❽ Le Vintage Bar/Café
❼ Hôtel Les Cascades	❾ Grocery
❽ Ibis Budget Hotel	⓴ Produits Regionaux Gribouille
❾ Le Fond de la Cour	
❿ La Cour Ste. Catherine & Travel Coffee Shop	㉑ Launderette
	㉒ Tourist Train Stop
⓫ Le Bacaretto	㉓ Art Gallery Row
⓬ Bistro des Artistes	㉔ Boat Tours (3)

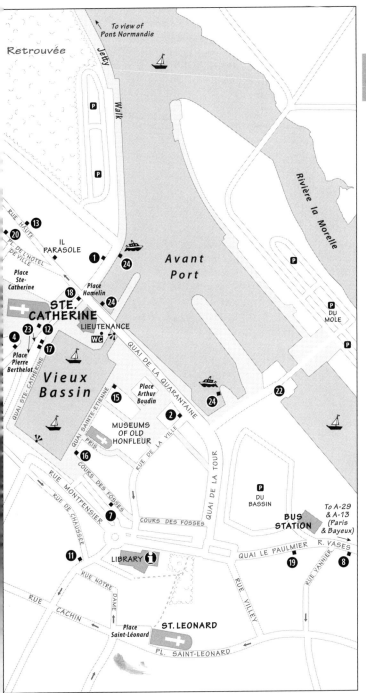

ARRIVAL IN HONFLEUR

By Bus: Get off at the small bus station *(gare routière),* and confirm your departure at the helpful information counter. To reach the TI and old town, turn right as you exit the station and walk five minutes up Quai le Paulmier. Note that the bus stop on Rue de la République may be more convenient for some accommodations.

By Car: Follow *Centre-Ville* signs, then find your hotel (easier said than done) and unload your bags (double-parking is OK for a few minutes). Parking is a headache in Honfleur, especially on summer and holiday weekends. Some hotels offer parking...for a price. Otherwise, your hotelier knows where you can park for free. If you don't mind paying for convenience, check first for a space in the small lot directly in front of the TI (€2/hour, €8/24 hours); if that's full, continue a couple of blocks farther to Parking du Bassin (€2/hour, €14/24 hours). Across the short causeway is Parking du Môle, which is cheaper (only €4/day), but a bit less central. Free parking is available at the Naturospace Museum, up Boulevard Charles V, near the beach. Parking Beaulieu is still farther (take Rue St-Nichol to Rue Guillaume de Beaulieu), but also free. Street parking, metered during the day, is free from 20:00 to 8:00.

HELPFUL HINTS

Museum Pass: The €10.20 museum pass, sold at participating museums, covers the Eugène Boudin Museum, Maisons Satie, and the Museums of Old Honfleur (Museum of the Navy and Museum of Ethnography and Norman Popular Art); it more than pays for itself with visits to the Boudin and Satie museums (www.musees-honfleur.fr).

Market Day: The area around Ste. Catherine Church becomes a colorful open-air market every Saturday (9:00-13:00). A smaller organic-food-only market takes place here on Wednesday mornings, and a flea market takes center stage here the first Sunday of every month and also on Wednesday evenings in summer.

Grocery Store: There's a grocery store near the TI with long hours (daily July-Aug, closed Mon off-season, 16 Quai le Paulmier).

Regional Products with Panache: Visit **Produits Regionaux Gribouille** for any Norman delicacy you can dream up. Say *bonjour* to Monsieur Gribouille (gree-boo-ee), and watch your head—his egg-beater collection hangs from above (Mon-Tue and Thu-Fri 9:30-12:45 & 14:00-18:30, Sat 9:30-19:00, Sun 10:00-18:00, closed Wed, 16 Rue de l'Homme de Bois, tel. 02 31 89 29 54).

Internet Access: Free Wi-Fi is available at the relaxed **Travel**

Coffee Shop (near the recommended La Cour Ste. Catherine B&B) and at several other cafés in town.

Laundry: La Lavandiere has handy drop-off service two blocks from the quaint harbor (Mon-Fri 9:00-19:00, Sat 10:00-20:00, closed Sun, 41 Rue de la République).

Taxi: Call mobile 06 08 60 17 98.

Tourist Train: Honfleur's *petit train* toots you up the Côte de Grâce—the hill overlooking the town—and back in about 45 minutes (€6.50, 4/day, more in summer, departs from across gray swivel bridge that leads to Parking du Môle).

Sights in Honfleur

▲▲Vieux Bassin

Stand near the water facing Honfleur's square harbor, with the merry-go-round across the lock to your left, and survey the town.

The word "Honfleur" is Scandinavian, meaning the shelter *(fleur)* of Hon (a Norse settler). This town has been sheltering residents for about a thousand years. During the Hundred Years' War (14th century), the entire harbor was fortified by a big wall with twin gatehouses (the one surviving gatehouse, La Lieutenance, is on your right). A narrow channel allowing boats to pass was protected by a heavy chain.

Those skinny houses on the right side were built for the town's fishermen and designed at a time when buildings were taxed based on their width, not height (and when knee replacements were unheard of). How about a room on the top floor, with no elevator? Imagine moving a piano or a refrigerator into one of these units today. The spire halfway up the left side of the port belongs to Honfleur's oldest church and is now home to the Marine Museum. The port, once crammed with fishing boats, now harbors sleek sailboats.

Walk toward the La Lieutenance gatehouse. In front of the barrel-vaulted arch (once the entry to the town), you can see a bronze bust of Samuel de Champlain—the explorer who sailed with an Honfleur crew 400 years ago to make his discoveries in Canada.

Turn around to see various tour and fishing boats and the masts of the high-flying Normandy Bridge (described later, under "Near Honfleur") in the distance. Fisherfolk catch flatfish, scallops, and tiny shrimp daily to bring to the Marché au Poisson, located toward the river (look for white metal structures with blue lettering). On the left you may see fishermen's wives selling *crevettes* (shrimp). You can buy them *cuites* (cooked) or *vivantes* (alive and wiggly). They are happy to let you sample one (rip off the cute little head and tail, and pop the middle into your mouth—*délicieuse!*), or buy a cupful to go for a few euros (daily in season).

You'll probably see artists sitting at easels around the harbor, as Boudin and Monet did. Many consider Honfleur the birthplace of 19th-century Impressionism. This was a time when people began to revere, not fear, the out-of-doors, and started to climb mountains "because they were there." Pretty towns like Honfleur and the nearby coast made perfect subjects to paint—and still are—thanks to what locals called the "unusual luminosity" of the region. And with the advent of trains in the late 1800s, artists could travel to the best light like never before. Artists would set up easels along the harbor to catch the light playing on the line of buildings, slate shingles, timbers, geraniums, clouds, and reflections in the water. Monet came here to visit the artist Boudin, a hometown boy, and the battle cry of the Impressionists—"Out of the studio and into the light!"—was born.

If you're an early riser, you can watch what's left of Honfleur's fishing fleet prepare for the day, and you just might experience that famous luminosity.

▲▲Ste. Catherine Church (Eglise Ste. Catherine)

The unusual wood-shingled exterior suggests that this church has a different story to tell than most. Walk inside. You'd swear that if it were turned over, it would float—the legacy of a community of sailors and fishermen, with loads of talented boat-builders and nary a cathedral architect. When workers put up the first nave in 1466, it soon became apparent that more space was needed—so the second was built in 1497. Because it felt too much like a market hall, they added side aisles. Notice the oak pillars, some full-length and others supported by stone bases. Trees come in different sizes, yet each pillar had to be the same thickness. In the last months of World War II, a bomb fell through the roof—but didn't explode. The pipe organ behind you is popular for concerts, and half of the modern pews are designed to flip so that you can face the music. Take a close look at the many medieval instruments carved into the railing below the organ—a 16th-century combo band in wood.

Cost and Hours: Free, daily July-Aug 9:00-18:30, Sept-June 9:00-17:15.

Bell Tower: The church's bell tower was built away from the church to avoid placing too much stress on the wooden church's roof, and to help minimize fire hazards (€2, free with ticket to the Eugène Boudin Museum, April-Sept Wed-Mon 10:00-12:00 & 14:00-18:00, closed Oct-March and Tue year-round). Historians consider the structure ugly—I like it. Notice the funky shingled chestnut beams that run from its squat base to support the skinny tower, and find the small, faded wooden sculpture of St. Catherine over the door. Go inside to appreciate the ancient wood framing and to see a good 15-minute video describing the bell tower's history. The highlights of the tiny museum are two wooden sculptures from the bows of two Louis XIII-era ships. Until recently the bell ringer lived in the bell tower (notice his fireplace behind the video area).

HONFLEUR'S MUSEUMS AND GALLERIES

Eugène Boudin ignited Honfleur's artistic tradition, which still burns today. The town is a popular haunt of artists, many of whom display their works in Honfleur's many art galleries (the best ones are along the streets between Ste. Catherine Church and the port). As you walk around the town visiting the museums, take time to enjoy today's art, too.

The €10.20 museum pass covers all four museums described below and pays for itself with visits to just the Boudin and Satie museums (pass sold at participating museums).

▲Eugène Boudin Museum

This pleasing little museum has three interesting floors with many paintings of Honfleur and the surrounding countryside. The first floor displays Norman folk costumes, the second floor has the Boudin collection, and the third floor houses the Hambourg/Rachet collection and the Katia Granoff room. The museum is in the midst of a multiyear renovation, so some sections (or even the entire museum) may be closed, and the locations of specific pieces will likely differ from what's described here—go with the flow.

Cost and Hours: €6, more during special exhibits, covered by museum pass; May-Sept Wed-Mon 10:00-12:00 & 14:00-18:00, closed Tue, shorter hours off-season; possibly closed for renovation in 2016; €2 English audioguide covers selected works (no English explanations on display—but none needed); elevator, no photos, Rue de l'Homme de Bois, tel. 02 31 89 54 00.

Visiting the Museum: Pick up a map at the ticket counter, tip your beret to Eugène Boudin, and climb the stairs (or take the elevator).

First Floor (Costumes): Monsieur and Madame Louveau (see their photo as you enter) gave Honfleur this quality collection of local traditional costumes. The hats, blouses, and shoes are supported by paintings that place them in an understandable historical and cultural context. Of special interest are the lace bonnets, typical of 19th-century Normandy. You could name a woman's village by her style of bonnet. The dolls are not toys for tots, but marketing

NORMANDY

Eugène Boudin (1824-1898)

Born in Honfleur, Boudin was the son of a harbor pilot. As an amateur teenage artist, he found work in an art-supply store that catered to famous artists from Paris (such as Jean-Baptiste-Camille Corot and Jean-François Millet) who came to paint the seaside. Boudin studied art in Paris but kept his hometown roots. Thanks to his Paris connections, Boudin's work was exhibited at the Paris salons.

At age 30 Boudin met the teenage Claude Monet. Monet had grown up in nearby Le Havre and, like Boudin, sketched the world around him—beaches, boats, and small-town life. Boudin encouraged him to don a scarf, set up his easel outdoors, and paint the scene exactly as he saw it. Today, we say: "Well, duh!" But "open-air" painting was unorthodox for artists trained to thoroughly study their subjects in the perfect lighting of a controlled studio setting. Boudin didn't teach Monet as much as give him the courage to follow his artistic instincts.

In the 1860s and 1870s, Boudin spent summers at his farm (St. Siméon) on the outskirts of Honfleur, hosting Monet, Edouard Manet, and other hangers-on. They taught Boudin the Impressionist techniques of using bright colors and building a subject with many individual brushstrokes. Boudin adapted those "strokes" to build subjects with "patches" of color. In 1874, Boudin joined the renegade Impressionists at their "revolutionary" exhibition in Paris.

tools for traveling clothing merchants—designed to show off the latest fashions. The men's department is in the back of the room.

Second Floor (Boudin Collection and More): Making a right off the stairs leads you into a large room of appealing 20th-century paintings and sculpture, created by artists who produced most of their works while living in Honfleur (special exhibits sometimes occupy this space). A left off the stairs leads through a temporary exhibition hall into the Salle Eugène Boudin, a small gallery of 19th-century paintings. In this room, Boudin's artwork is mixed with that of his colleagues and contemporaries; paintings by Claude Monet and Gustave Courbet are usually displayed, letting you see how those masters took Boudin's approach to the next level, with rougher brushstrokes and even more abstraction. Find the glass display case in the rear titled *Précurseur de l'Impressionisme*, with little pastel drawings, and follow Boudin's art chronologically, as it evolves, from Romanticism through Realism to Impressionism (the heart of this museum).

Upon showing their work in Paris, local artists—such as Eugène Boudin—created enough of a stir that Normandy came into vogue; many Parisian artists (including Monet and other early Impressionists) traveled to Honfleur to dial in to the action. Boudin himself made a big impression on the father of Impressionism by introducing Monet to the practice of painting outside. This collection of Boudin's paintings—which the artist gave to his hometown—shows how his technique developed, from realistic portrayals of subjects (outlines colored in, like a coloring book) to masses of colors catching light (Impressionism). Boudin's beach scenes, showing aristocrats taking a healthy saltwater dip, helped fuel that style. His skies were good enough to earn him the nickname "King of Skies."

Third Floor (Hambourg/Rachet Collection): Follow the steps that lead from the Boudin room to the small Hambourg/Rachet collection (and a smashing painting of Honfleur at twilight). In 1988, André Hambourg and his wife, Nicole Rachet, donated their art to this museum. The collection is enjoyably Impressionistic, but largely from the mid-20th century.

Third Floor (Salle Katia Granoff): Retrace your steps back to the main stairway to reach the other third-floor room, where you'll find a worthwhile collection of 20th-century works by artists who lived and learned in Honfleur. Find the few paintings by Raoul Dufy (a French Fauvist painter), and compare his imaginative scenes of Normandy with others you've seen. And remember, just because you may not recognize an artist's name doesn't mean that you can't enjoy the work. Be sure to take in the brilliant view of the Normandy Bridge through the windows.

▲Maisons Satie

If Honfleur is over-the-top cute, this museum, housed in composer Erik Satie's birthplace, is a burst of witty charm—just like the musical genius it honors. While enjoyable for Satie's fans, it can be a ho-hum experience for those unfamiliar with Satie and his music.

Cost and Hours: €6.10, covered by museum pass; May-Sept Wed-Mon 10:00-19:00; Oct-Dec and mid-Feb-April Wed-Mon 11:00-18:00; closed Jan-mid-Feb and Tue year-round; last entry one hour before closing, includes audioguide, 5-minute walk from harbor at 67 Boulevard Charles V, tel. 02 31 89 11 11, www.musees-honfleur.fr.

Visiting the Museum: As you wander from room to room with your included audioguide, infrared signals transmit bits of Satie's minimalist music, along with a first-person story (in English). As if you're living as an artist in 1920s Paris, you'll drift past winged pears, strangers in the window, and small girls with green eyes. (If you like what you hear...don't move; the infrared transmission is hypersensitive, and the soundtrack switches every few feet.) The finale—performed by you—is the *Laboratory of Emotions* pedal-go-round, a self-propelled carousel where your feet create

NORMANDY

the music (be sure to pedal softly). For a relaxing break, enjoy the 12-minute movie (4/hour, French only) featuring modern dance springing from *Parade,* Satie's collaboration with Pablo Picasso and Jean Cocteau; the Dadaist *Relâche;* and other works. You'll even hear the boos and whistles that greeted these ballets' debuts.

Museums of Old Honfleur

Two side-by-side folk museums combine to paint a picture of daily life in Honfleur during the time when its ships were king and the city had global significance. The curator creatively supports the artifacts with paintings, making the cultural context clearer. Both museums have loaner handouts with English explanations.

Cost and Hours: €4 each or €5.20 for both, covered by museum pass; Tue-Sun 10:00-12:00 & 14:00-18:30, shorter hours off-season; closed mid-Nov-mid-Feb and Mon year-round.

Visiting the Museums: Facing the port, the skippable **Museum of the Sea** (Musée de la Marine) fills Honfleur's oldest church (15th century) with a cool collection of models from fishing boats to naval ships (many of which were constructed in Honfleur's shipyards), marine paraphernalia, and paintings.

The more engaging **Museum of Ethnography and Norman Popular Art** (Musée d'Ethnographie et d'Art Populaire), located in the old prison and courthouse, re-creates typical rooms from Honfleur's past and crams them with objects of daily life—costumes, furniture, looms, and an antique printing press. You'll see the old yard, climb through two stories of furnished rooms, and wind up in the old-time, street-level shop.

HONFLEUR WALKS
▲Côte de Grâce Walk

For good exercise and a bird's-eye view of Honfleur and the Normandy Bridge, take the steep 20-minute walk (or quick drive) up to the Côte de Grâce—best in the early morning or at sunset. From Ste. Catherine Church, walk or drive up Rue du Puits, then follow the blue-on-white signs to reach the splendid view over Honfleur at the top of the ramp (benches and information plaque). *Piétons* (walkers) should veer right up La Rampe du Mont Joli; *conducteurs* (drivers) should keep straight. Walkers can continue past the view for about 300 yards to the **Chapel of Notre-Dame de Grâce.** Built in the early 1600s by the mariners and people of Honfleur, the church oozes seafaring mementos. Model boats hang from the ceiling, pictures of boats balance high on the walls, and several stained-glass windows are decorated with images of sailors praying to the Virgin Mary while at sea. Even the holy water basins to the left and right of the entrance are in the shape of seashells. Find the church bells hanging on a wood rack to the right as you leave the church and imagine the racket they could make (daily 8:30-17:15).

Below the chapel, a lookout offers a sweeping view of super-industrial Le Havre, with the Manche (English Channel) to your left and the (just visible) Normandy Bridge to your right.

Jetty/Park Walk

Take a level stroll in Honfleur along the water past the Hôtel le Cheval Blanc to find the mouth of the Seine River and big ships at sea. You'll pass kid-friendly parks carpeted with flowers and grass, and continue past the lock connecting Honfleur to the Seine and the sea. Grand and breezy vistas of the sea and smashing views of the Normandy Bridge reward the diligent walker (allow 20 minutes from the harbor to reach the best views).

NEAR HONFLEUR

Boat Excursions

Boat trips in and around Honfleur depart from various docks between Hôtel le Cheval Blanc and the opposite end of the outer port (Easter-Oct usually about 11:00-17:00). The tour boat *Calypso* takes good 45-minute spins around Honfleur's harbor (€6, mobile 06 71 64 50 46). Other cruises run to the Normandy Bridge (described next), which, unfortunately, means two boring trips through the locks (€9.50/1.5 hours, choose between *Jolie France*, mobile 06 71 64 50 46, or *Les Vedettes Cauchois* near Hôtel le Cheval Blanc, mobile 06 31 89 21 10).

Normandy Bridge (Pont de Normandie)

The 1.25-mile-long Normandy Bridge is the longest cable-stayed bridge in the Western world (€5.40 toll each way, not worth a detour). This is a key piece of European expressway that links the Atlantic ports from Belgium to Spain. View the bridge from Honfleur (better from an excursion boat or the Jetty Walk described earlier, and best at night, when bridge is floodlit). Also consider visiting the bridge's free Exhibition Hall (under tollbooth on Le Havre side, daily 8:00-19:00). The Seine finishes its winding 500-mile journey here, dropping only 1,500 feet from its source, 450 miles away. The river flows so slowly that, in certain places, a stiff breeze can send it flowing upstream.

▲Etrétat

France's answer to the White Cliffs of Dover, these chalky cliffs soar high above a calm, crescent beach (from Honfleur, it's about 50 minutes by car or 2 hours by bus via Le Havre). Walking trails lead hikers from the small seaside resort of Etrétat along a vertiginous route with sensational views (and crowds of hikers in summer and on weekends). You'll recognize these cliffs—and the arches and stone spire that decorate them—from countless Impressionist paintings, including several at the Eugène Boudin Museum in Honfleur. The small, Coney Island-like town holds plenty of cafés and a **TI** (Place Maurice Guillard, tel. 02 35 27 05 21, www.etretat.net).

Getting There: Etrétat is north of Le Havre. To get here by car, cross the Normandy Bridge and follow A-29, then exit at *sortie Etrétat.* Buses serve Etrétat from Le Havre's *gare routière,* adjacent to the train station (5/day, 1 hour, www.keolis-seine-maritime.com).

Sleeping in Etrétat: **$$$ Dormy House** has a brilliant setting and makes a nice splurge if the scenery moves you (Db-€140-350, Route du Havre at the edge of Etrétat, tel. 02 35 27 07 88, www.dormy-house.com, info@etretat-hotel.com).

Sleeping in Honfleur

Though Honfleur is popular in summer, it's busiest on weekends and holidays (blame Paris). English is widely spoken (blame vacationing Brits). A few moderate accommodations remain, but most hotels are pretty pricey. Only two hotels have elevators (Hôtel le Cheval Blanc and Ibis Budget Honfleur), but Hotel Monet has ground-floor rooms.

HOTELS

$$$ L'Absinthe Hôtel*** offers 11 stylish, tastefully restored rooms with king-size beds in two locations. Rooms in the main (reception) section come with wood-beamed decor and Jacuzzi tubs, and share a cozy public lounge with a fireplace (Db-€160-210). Five rooms are located above their next-door restaurant and have views of the modern port and three-star, state-of-the-art comfort (Db-€170-190, Db suite-€265; breakfast-€13, air-con in both buildings, private parking-€13/day, 1 Rue de la Ville, tel. 02 31 89 23 23, www.absinthe.fr, reservation@absinthe.fr).

$$$ Hôtel le Cheval Blanc***, a Best Western, is a waterfront splurge with port views from all of its 35 plush and pricey rooms (many with queen-size beds), plus a rare-in-this-town elevator and a spa, but no air-conditioning—noise can be a problem with windows open (small Db with lesser view-€155, Db with full port view-€180-230, family rooms/suites-€280-435, breakfast-€13, 2 Quai des Passagers, tel. 02 31 81 65 00, www.hotel-honfleur.com, info@hotel-honfleur.com).

$$$ Hôtel de l'Ecrin*** is a true Old World refuge. Enter the private courtyard to find a vintage mansion anchoring a sprawling compound with immaculate gardens around ample grass, a big pool, a sauna and Jacuzzi, and creaky old public spaces Eugène

Boudin would appreciate. The 34 rooms have a faded elegance and are *très* traditional—some have four-poster *grand lits* (Db-€120, bigger Db-€149-180, big suites-€200-250, continental breakfast-€11, buffet breakfast-€15, free and secure parking, 10 minutes by foot from the harbor at 19 Rue Eugène Boudin, tel. 02 31 14 43 45, www.honfleur.com, hotel.ecrin@honfleur.com).

$$$ **Hôtel du Dauphin***** is centrally located, with a colorful lounge/breakfast room, many narrow stairs (normal in Honfleur),

and an Escher-esque floor plan. The 30 mostly smallish rooms— some with open-beam ceilings, some with queen- or king-size beds—provide reasonable comfort for the price. If you need a lower floor or bigger bed, request it when you book (Db-€75-129 depending on size of bed and view, Tb-€159, Qb-€165-179, breakfast-€13, Wi-Fi in lobby only, a stone's throw from Ste. Catherine Church at 10 Place Pierre Berthelot, tel. 02 31 89 15 53, www.hoteldudauphin.com, info@hoteldudauphin. com). The same owners also run the $$$ **Hôtel des Loges*****, a few doors up, which offers larger rooms with Wi-Fi, but less personality (Db-€109-118). Both hotels offer the first breakfast free for Rick Steves readers in 2016 if you book direct—mention when you reserve and show this book at check-in.

$$ **Hôtel Monet****, on the road to the Côte de Grâce and a 10-minute walk down to the port (longer back up), is an overlooked find. This tranquil spot houses 16 mostly tight but good-value rooms facing a courtyard, many with a patio made for picnics. You'll meet welcoming owners Christophe and Sylvie (Db-€82-120, Tb-€99-140, Qb-€110-160, highest rates are for July-Sept, breakfast-€10, free and easy parking, Charrière du Puits, tel. 02 31 89 00 90, www.hotel-monet-honfleur.com, contact@hotel-monet-honfleur.com). Reception is closed from 13:00-17:00.

$$ **Hôtel Les Cascades,** across from the TI and a few blocks from the bus station, delivers basic comfort in a central location at fair prices. The 17 rooms have only double beds (some with two) and the hotel plays second fiddle to its restaurant, so don't expect attentive service (Db-€80-95, breakfast-€9, 19 Cours des Fossés, tel. 02 31 89 05 83, www.lescascades.com, info@lescascades.com).

$ **Ibis Budget Honfleur** is modern, efficient, trim, and cheap, with prefab bathrooms and an antiseptically clean ambience (Db/Tb-€52 on weekdays, €60 on weekends, cheaper off-season, breakfast-€7, reception closed 21:00-6:00 but automatic check-in with credit card available 24 hours, elevator, across from bus station and main parking lot on Rue des Vases, tel. 08 92 68 07 81, www. ibisbudget.com, h2716-re@accor.com).

CHAMBRES D'HOTES

The TI has a long list of Honfleur's many *chambres d'hôtes* (rooms in private homes), but most are too far from the town center. Those listed here are good values.

$$$ At Le Fond de la Cour, British expats Amanda and Craig offer a good mix of crisp, modern, and comfortable accommodations around a peaceful courtyard. There's a large cottage that can sleep four, two apartments with small kitchens, and three standard doubles (Db-€95-145, Tb-€130-160, price depends on size, extra person-€30, short apartment stays possible, standard rooms include English-style breakfast, apartment dwellers also get free breakfast with this book, free street parking, limited private parking-€10/day, 29 Rue Eugène Boudin, mobile 06 72 20 72 98, www. lefonddelacour.com, amanda.ferguson@orange.fr).

$$ La Cour Ste. Catherine, kitty-corner to Le Fond de la Cour, is an enchanting bed-and-breakfast run by the openhearted Madame Giaglis ("call me Liliane") and her big-hearted husband, Monsieur Liliane (a.k.a. Antoine). Their six big, modern rooms—each with firm beds and a separate sitting area—surround a perfectly Norman courtyard with a small terrace, fine plantings, and a cozy lounge area ideal for cool evenings. The rooms are as cheery as the owner—ask about her coffee shop (Db-€90, Db suite-€140, Tb/Qb-€150, extra bed-€30, includes breakfast, small apartments that sleep up to 6 and cottage with kitchen also available, cash only, free parking in 2016 with this book when you book direct, 200 yards up Rue du Puits from Ste. Catherine Church at #74, tel. 02 31 89 42 40, www.coursaintecatherine.com, coursaintecatherine@ orange.fr).

Eating in Honfleur

Eat seafood or cream sauces here. It's a tough choice between the irresistible waterfront tables of the many look-alike places lining the harbor and the eateries with good reputations elsewhere in town. Trust my dinner suggestions and consider your hotelier's opinion. It's best to call ahead to reserve at most restaurants in Honfleur (particularly on weekends).

Le Bouilland Normand hides a block off the port on a pleasing square and offers a true Norman experience at reasonable prices. Claire and chef-hubby Bruno provide quality *Normand* cuisine and enjoy serving travelers. Daily specials complement the classic offerings (€22-30 *menus*, closed Wed, dine inside or out, 7 Rue de la Ville, tel. 02 31 89 02 41, www.aubouillonnormand.fr).

Le Bacaretto wine bar-café is run by laid-back Hervé, the antithesis of a wine snob. This relaxed, tiny, wine-soaked place offers a fine selection of wines by the glass at good prices and a small but appealing assortment of appetizers and *plats du jour* that can make a full meal (closed Wed-Thu for lunch and Sun for dinner, 44 Rue de la Chaussée, tel. 02 31 14 83 11).

Bistro des Artistes is a two-woman operation and the joy of locals (call ahead for a window table). Hardworking Anne-Marie cooks from a select repertoire upstairs while her server takes care of business in the pleasant little dining room. Portions are huge and very homemade; order only one course and maybe a dessert (€19-28 *plats,* closed Wed, 30 Place Berthelot, tel. 02 31 89 95 90).

Au P'tit Mareyeur is whisper-formal, intimate, all about seafood, and a good value. The ground floor and upstairs rooms offer equal comfort and ambience (€35 four-course *menu,* €35 famous Bouillabaisse Honfleuraise, closed Tue-Wed and Jan, 4 Rue Haute, tel. 02 31 98 84 23, mobile 06 84 33 24 03, www.auptitmareyeur.fr, friendly owner Julie speaks some English).

L'Homme de Bois combines way-cozy ambience with authentic Norman cuisine and good prices (€23 three-course *menu* with few choices, €26-36 *menus* give more choices, daily, a few outside tables, 30 Rue de l'Homme de Bois, tel. 02 31 89 75 27).

Travel Coffee Shop is an ideal breakfast or lunch option for travelers wanting conversation—in either English or French—and good food at very fair prices (May-Sept Thu-Tue 8:00-17:00, closed Wed; April and Oct-Nov Sat-Sun only, closed Dec-March; 6 Place du Puits).

Dining Along the Harbor: If the weather cooperates, slide down to the harbor and table-shop the joints that line the high side. Several places have effective propane heaters. Although the cuisine is mostly mediocre, the setting is uniquely Honfleur—and, on a languid evening, hard to pass up. Take a stroll along the port and compare restaurant views, chair comfort, and menu selection (all of these places look the same to me). If you dine elsewhere, come here for a before- or after-dinner drink. Of the harborfront options, **Café de l'Hôtel de Ville** owns the best afternoon sun exposure (and charges for it) and looks across to Honfleur's soaring homes (open daily July-Aug, closed Tue off-season, Place de l'Hôtel de Ville, tel. 02 31 89 07 29).

Breakfast: If it's even close to sunny, skip your hotel breakfast and enjoy ambience for a cheaper price by eating on the port, where several cafés offer *petit déjeuner* (€3-7 for continental fare, €7-13 for more elaborate choices). Morning sun and views are best from the high side of the harbor. Or, if price or companionship matter, head to the Travel Coffee Shop for the best breakfast deal in town (described earlier).

Dessert: Honfleur is ice-cream crazy, with gelato and traditional ice-cream shops on every corner. If you need a Ben & Jerry's ice-cream fix or a scrumptious dessert crêpe, find the **waterfront stand** at the southeast corner of the Vieux Bassin.

Nighttime Food to Go: Order a tasty pizza to go until late from **Il Parasole** (2 Rue Haute, tel. 02 31 98 94 29), and enjoy a picnic dinner with port views a few steps away in front of the La Lieutenance gatehouse.

Nightlife: Nightlife in Honfleur centers on the old port. Several bar/cafés line the high-building side of the port. These two are Honfleur's down-and-dirty watering holes: **L'Albatross** (pub-like with flags, banners, and a loyal following—including me) and **Le Perroquet Vert** (also cool but more existential—"those lights are so..."). **Le Vintage,** just off the port, is a happening bar/café with live piano and jazz on weekend nights. Casual outdoor seating and a vigorous interior make this a fun choice (closed Tue, 8 Quai des Passagers, tel. 02 31 89 05 28).

Honfleur Connections

There's no direct train service to Honfleur, so you must take a bus to or from a city with rail service. The express PrestoBus—line #39—which links Honfleur with Caen and Le Havre is handy, but runs only two or three times a day. Nonexpress bus routes also connect Honfleur with Le Havre, Caen, Deauville, and Lisieux—all with direct rail service to Paris. Bus #50 runs between Le Havre, Honfleur and Lisieux; bus #20 connects Le Havre, Honfleur, Deauville, and Caen. Although train and bus service usually are coordinated, confirm your connection with the helpful staff at Honfleur's bus station (English info desk open Mon-Fri 9:30-12:00 & 13:00-18:00, in summer also Sat-Sun, tel. 02 31 89 28 41, www.busverts.fr). If the station is closed, you can get schedules at the TI. Railpass holders will save money by connecting through Deauville, as bus fares increase with distance (Deauville to Honfleur-€2.40, Lisieux to Honfleur-€4.70).

From Honfleur by Bus and/or Train to: Caen (express PrestoBus 2-3/day, 1 hour; more scenic *par la côte* bus #20 4/day direct, 2 hours); **Bayeux** (2-3/day, 1.5 hours; first take PrestoBus to Caen, then 20-minute train to Bayeux, more via scenic bus #20 via the coast to Caen); **Rouen** (6/day Mon-Sat, 3/day Sun, bus-and-train combo involves 30-minute bus ride over Normandy Bridge to Le Havre, then easy transfer to 1-hour train to Rouen); **Paris'** Gare St. Lazare (13/day, 2.5-3.5 hours, by bus to Caen, Lisieux, Deauville, or Le Havre, then train to Paris; buses from Honfleur meet most Paris trains).

Route Tips for Drivers: If connecting to the D-Day beaches, consider taking the scenic route *"par la Côte"* to Trouville and pass sea views, thatched hamlets, and stupendous mansions. From Honfleur, drive to the port, pass Hôtel du Cheval Blanc, and stick to this road (D-513) to Trouville, then follow signs for A-13 to Caen.

Bayeux

Only six miles from the D-Day beaches, Bayeux was the first city liberated after the landing. Incredibly, the town was spared the bombs of World War II. After a local chaplain made sure London knew that his city was not a German headquarters and was of no strategic importance, a scheduled bombing raid was canceled—making Bayeux the closest city to the D-Day landing site not destroyed. Even without its famous medieval tapestry and proximity to the D-Day beaches, Bayeux would be worth a visit for its enjoyable town center and awe-inspiring cathedral, beautifully illuminated at night. Its location and manageable size (pop. 14,000) makes Bayeux an ideal home base for visiting the area's sights, particularly if you lack a car.

Orientation to Bayeux

TOURIST INFORMATION

The TI is on a small bridge two blocks north of the cathedral. Ask for the free *D-Day Normandy* booklet, bus schedules to the beaches, and regional information, and inquire about special events and concerts (June-Aug Mon-Sat 9:00-19:00, Sun 9:00-13:00 & 14:00-18:00; April-May and Sept-Oct Mon-Sat 9:30-12:30 & 14:00-18:00, Sun 10:00-13:00 & 14:00-18:00; shorter hours off-season; on Pont St. Jean leading to Rue St. Jean, tel. 02 31 51 28 28, www.bessin-normandie.com).

For a **self-guided walking tour,** pick up the map called *Découvrez Vieux Bayeux* at the TI. Follow the bronze plates embedded in the sidewalk, and look for information plaques with English translations that correspond to your map.

ARRIVAL IN BAYEUX

By Train and Bus: Trains and buses share the same station (no bag storage). It's a 15-minute walk from the station to the tapestry, and 15 minutes from the tapestry to Place St. Patrice (and several recommended hotels). To reach the tapestry, the cathedral, and the hotels, cross the major street in front of the station and follow Rue de Cremel toward *l'Hôpital*, then turn left on Rue Nesmond. Find

NORMANDY

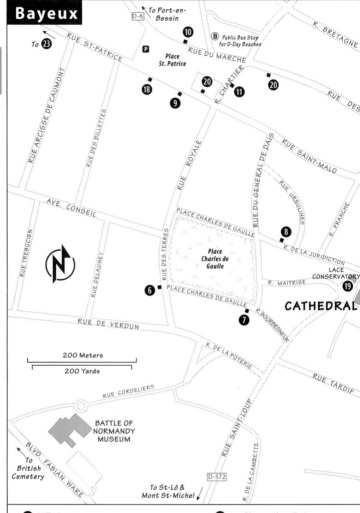

Bayeux

To Port-en-Bessin

To ②

RUE ST-PATRICE

Place St. Patrice

RUE DU MARCHE

⑩

Ⓑ Public Bus Stop for D-Day Beaches

R. BRETAGNE

RUE ARCISSE DE CAUMONT

RUE DES BILLETTES

⑱

⑨

R. CHARTIER

⑳

⑪

⑳

RUE DES

AVE. CONSEIL

RUE TREBUCIEN

RUE DELAUNEY

RUE ROYALE

RUE DES TERRES

PLACE CHARLES DE GAULLE

Place Charles de Gaulle

RUE SAINT-MALO

RUE DU GENERAL DE DAIS

RUE URSULINES

RUE FRANCHE

⑧

R. DE LA JURIDICTION

LACE CONSERVATORY

⑲

R. MAITRISE

CATHEDRAL

⑥

PLACE CHARLES DE GAULLE

⑦

R. BOURBESNEUR

RUE DE VERDUN

R. DE LA POTERIE

200 Meters

200 Yards

RUE CORDELIERS

RUE TARDIF

BATTLE OF NORMANDY MUSEUM

RUE SAINT-LOUP

BLVD. FABIAN WARE

To British Cemetery

D-572

R. DE LA CAMBETTE

To St-Lô & Mont St-Michel

① Villa Lara
② Hôtel Churchill & Carrefour City Grocery
③ Hôtel le Lion d'Or
④ Hôtel Reine Mathilde & Le Garde Manger
⑤ Hôtel au Georges VII & Café
⑥ Le Petit Matin
⑦ Logis les Remparts B&B
⑧ Manoir Sainte Victoire
⑨ Hôtel d'Argouges
⑩ Hôtel de Sainte Croix
⑪ Hôtel Mogador

⑫ La Chaumière Deli
⑬ La Rapière Restaurant
⑭ Le Volet Qui Penche
⑮ L'Angle Saint Laurent
⑯ Le Pommier Restaurant
⑰ Au P'tit Bistrot
⑱ Taverne des Ducs
⑲ Lace Conservatory
⑳ Launderettes (3)
㉑ Bike Rental
㉒ Renault Car Rental
㉓ To Hertz Car Rental

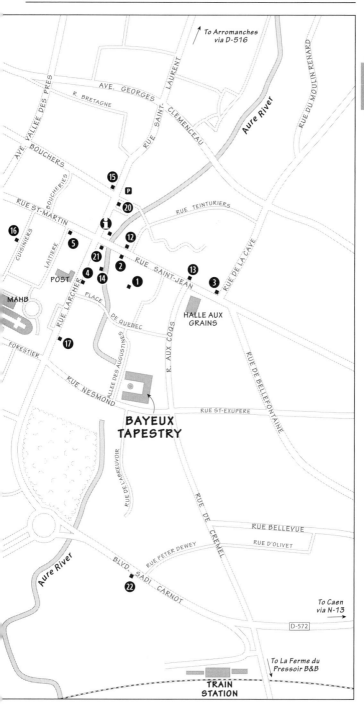

signs to the *Tapisserie* or continue on to the cathedral. Taxis are usually waiting at the station. Allow €8 for a taxi from the train station to any recommended hotel or sight in Bayeux, and €21 to Arromanches (€32 after 19:00 and on Sundays, taxi tel. 02 31 92 92 40 or mobile 06 70 40 07 96).

By Car: Look for the cathedral spires and follow signs for *Centre-Ville,* and then signs for the *Tapisserie* (tapestry) or your hotel (individual hotels are well-signed from the ring road—wait for yours to appear). Day-trippers will find pay parking lots in the town center (including at the Hôtel de Ville near the TI, and at Place St. Patrice; €1/hour, 3-hour limit). A few other parking lots are free but require a cardboard clock on your dashboard and are limited to four hours. (Note that these time limits are not enforced from 12:00 to 14:00, allowing you to stretch your stay.) To park for longer, you can find free, unlimited lots along the southern ring road (along Boulevard Marechal Leclerc and Boulevard Sadi Carnot).

Drivers connecting Bayeux with Mont St-Michel should use the speedy, free A-84 autoroute.

HELPFUL HINTS

Market Days: The Saturday open-air market on Place St. Patrice is Bayeux's best, though the Wednesday market on pedestrian Rue St. Jean is pleasant. Both end by 13:00. Don't leave your car on Place St. Patrice on a Friday night, as it will be towed early Saturday.

Grocery Store: Carrefour City, at Rue St. Jean 14, is next to the recommended Hôtel Churchill (Mon-Sat 7:00-22:00, Sun 9:00-22:00).

Internet Access: The recommended **Le Garde Manger** café has free Wi-Fi for customers.

Laundry: A launderette with big machines is a block behind the TI, on Rue Maréchal Foch. Two more launderettes are near Place St. Patrice: One is at 4 Rue St. Patrice and the other is at 69 Rue des Bouchers (all open daily 7:00-21:00).

Bike Rental: Vélos Location has what you need and will deliver to outlying hotels (daily April-Oct 8:00-20:30, closes earlier off-season, inside grocery store across from TI at Impasse de Islet, tel. 02 31 92 89 16, www.velosbayeux.com).

Taxi: Call 02 31 92 92 40 or mobile 06 70 40 07 96.

Car Rental: Bayeux offers a few choices. **Renault Rent** is handiest, just below the train station at the BP gas station. A rental at about €70/day with a 200-kilometer limit is sufficient to see the key sights from Arromanches to Utah Beach—you'll drive about 180 kilometers (16 Boulevard Sadi Carnot, tel. 02 31

51 18 51). **Hertz** is the only agency in town that allows you to drop off in a different city (located west of the city center on Route de Cherbourg, off D-613, tel. 02 31 92 03 26).

Sights in Bayeux

Bayeux's three main museums—the Bayeux Tapestry, Battle of Normandy Memorial Museum, and MAHB—offer combo-tickets that will save you money if you plan to see more than one sight. Combo-tickets covering two sights cost €12; for all three it's €15 (buy the combo-ticket at the first sight you visit).

▲▲▲Bayeux Tapestry (Tapisserie de Bayeux)

Made of wool embroidered onto linen cloth, this historically precious document is a mesmerizing 70-yard-long cartoon. The tapestry tells the story of William the Conqueror's rise from duke of Normandy to king of England, and shows his victory over England's King Harold at the Battle of Hastings in 1066. Long and skinny, the tapestry was designed to hang in the nave of Bayeux's cathedral as a reminder for locals of their ancestor's courage. The terrific museum that houses the tapestry is an unusually good chance to teach your kids about the Middle Ages: Models, mannequins, a movie, and more make it an engaging, fun place to visit.

Cost and Hours: €9, combo-ticket with other Bayeux museums-€12 or €15, includes excellent audioguide for adults and a special kids' version, daily May-Aug 9:00-19:00, March-April and Sept-Oct 9:00-18:30, Nov-Feb 9:30-12:30 & 14:00-18:00, last entry 45 minutes before closing, tel. 02 31 51 25 50, www.bayeuxmuseum.com.

Crowd-Beating Tips: To avoid crowds, arrive before 10:00 or late in the day. It's busiest in August, and most crowded from 10:00 to 17:00.

Film: When buying your ticket, ask when they'll show the English version of the 16-minute battle film (runs every 40 minutes, English times also posted at the base of the steps to the theater).

Visiting the Museum: Your visit has three separate parts that tell the basic story of the Battle of Hastings, provide historical context for the event, and explain how the tapestry was made. At a minimum, allow a full hour to appreciate this important artifact.

Bayeux History—The Battle of Hastings

Because of this pivotal battle, the most memorable date of the Middle Ages is 1066. England's king, Edward the Confessor, was about to die without an heir. The big question: Who would succeed him—Harold, an English nobleman and the king's brother-in-law, or William, duke of Normandy and the king's cousin? Edward chose William, and sent Harold to Normandy to give William the news. On the journey, Harold was captured. To win his release, he promised he would be loyal to William and not contest the decision. To test his loyalty, William sent Harold to battle for him in Brittany. Harold was successful, and William knighted him. To further test his loyalty, William had Harold swear on the relics of the Bayeux cathedral that when Edward died, he would allow William to ascend the throne. Harold returned to England, Edward died...and Harold grabbed the throne.

William, known as William the Bastard, invaded England to claim the throne. Harold met him in southern England at the town of Hastings, where their forces fought a fierce 14-hour battle. Harold was killed, and his Saxon forces were routed. William—now "the Conqueror"—marched to London, claimed his throne, and became king of England (though he spoke no English) as well as duke of Normandy.

The advent of a Norman king of England muddied the political waters and set in motion 400 years of conflict between England and France—not to be resolved until the end of the Hundred Years' War (1453). The Norman conquest of England brought that country into the European mainstream (but still no euros). The Normans established a strong central English government. Historians speculate that had William not succeeded, England would have remained on the fringe of Europe (like Scandinavia), and French culture (and language) would have prevailed in the New World—which would have meant no communication issues for us in France. Hmmm.

Your visit starts with the actual **tapestry,** accompanied by an included audioguide that gives a top-notch, fast-moving, 20-minute scene-by-scene narration complete with period music (if you lose your place, find subtitles in Latin). To keep crowds moving from May through September, the audioguide's pause and rewind functions are disabled, though these are helpful to use off-season. Appreciate the fun details—such as the bare legs in scene 4 or Harold's pouting expressions in various frames—and look for references to places you may have visited (like Dinan). Pay strict attention to scene 23, where Harold takes his oath to William; the importance of keeping one's word is the point of the tapestry. Get close and (almost) feel the tapestry's texture.

Next you'll climb upstairs into a room filled with engaging **exhibits**, including a full-size replica of a Viking ship much like the one William used to cross the Channel (Normans inherited their weaponry and seafaring skills from the Norsemen). You'll also see mannequins (find William looking unmoved with his new crown), a replica of the Domesday Book (an inventory of noble's lands as ordered by William), and models of castles (who knew that the Tower of London was a Norman project?). Good explanations outline the events surrounding the invasion and the subsequent creation of the tapestry, and a touchscreen lets you see the back side of the embroidery.

Your visit finishes with a 16-minute **film** that ties it all together one last time (in the cinema upstairs, skippable if you're pressed for time). You'll exit below, through a *formidable* boutique.

Remember, this is Norman propaganda: The English (the bad guys, referred to as *les goddamns,* after a phrase the French kept hearing them say) are shown with mustaches and long hair; the French (*les* good guys) are clean-cut and clean-shaven—with even the backs of their heads shaved for a better helmet fit.

▲Bayeux Cathedral

This massive building, as big as Paris' Notre-Dame, dominates the small town of Bayeux. (Make it a point to see the cathedral after dark, when it's beautifully illuminated.)

Cost and Hours: Free, daily July-Aug 8:30-19:00, Sept-June 8:30-18:00.

Visiting the Cathedral: To start your visit, find the small **square** opposite the front entry (information board about the cathedral in rear corner). Notice the two dark towers—originally Romanesque, they were capped later with tall Gothic spires. The cathedral's west facade is structurally Romanesque, but with a decorative Gothic "curtain" added.

Before entering, head just to the left of the cathedral, find the stairs at the top of a walking lane, and crane your neck up. The little rectangular stone house atop the near tower was the **watchman's home,** from which he'd keep an eye out for incoming English troops during the Hundred Years' War...and for Germans five centuries later (it didn't work—the Germans took the town in 1940). Bayeux was liberated on D-Day plus one: June 7. About the only casualty was the German lookout—shot while doing just that from the window of this stone house.

Now step inside the cathedral. The magnificent view of the **nave** from the top of the steps shows a mix of Romanesque (ground floor) and soaring Gothic (upper floors). Historians believe the Bayeux tapestry originally hung here. Imagine it hanging halfway up the big Romanesque arches. This section is brightly lit by the huge windows above. Try to visualize this scene with the original, richly colored stained glass in all those upper windows. Rare 13th-century stained-glass bits are in the high central window above the altar; the other stained glass is from the 19th and 20th centuries.

Walk down the nave and notice the areas between the big, round **arches**. That busy zigzag patterning characterizes Norman art in France as well as in England. These 11th-century Romanesque arches are decorated with a manic mix of repeated geometric shapes: half-circles, hash marks, full circles, and diagonal lines. Notice also the creepy faces eyeing you, especially the ring of devil heads three arches up on the right. Yuck.

Information panels in the side aisles give basic facts about the cathedral (in English). More 13th-century Norman Gothic is in the choir (the fancy area behind the central altar). Here, simple Romanesque carvings lie under Gothic arches with characteristic tall, thin lines adding a graceful verticality to the overall feel of the interior.

For maximum 1066 atmosphere, step into the spooky **crypt** (beneath the central altar), which was used originally as a safe spot for the cathedral's relics. The crypt displays two freestanding columns and bulky capitals with fine Romanesque carving. During a reinforcement of the nave, these two columns were replaced. Workers removed the Gothic veneer and discovered their true inner Romanesque beauty. Orange angel-musicians on other columns add color to this somber room.

River Walk

Join the locals and promenade along the meandering walking path that follows the little Aure River for about 2.5 miles through Bayeux. The path runs both ways from the TI (find the waterwheel behind the TI and keep walking; path marked on city maps).

Lace Conservatory (Conservatoire de Dentelles)

Notable for its carved 15th-century facade, the Adam and Eve house (find Adam, Eve, and the snake) offers a chance to watch workers design and weave intricate lace, just as artisans did in the 1600s. Enter to the clicking sound of the small wooden bobbins used by the lacemakers, and appreciate the concentration that their work requires. You can also see examples of lace from the past and pick up some nifty souvenirs.

Cost and Hours: Free, Mon-Sat 9:30-12:30 & 14:30-18:00 except Mon and Thu until 17:00, closed Sun, across from cathedral entrance, tel. 02 31 92 73 80, http://dentelledebayeux.free.fr.

MAHB (Musée d'Art et d'Histoire Baron Gérard)

For a break from D-Day and tapestries, MAHB offers a modest review of European art and history in what was once the Bayeux bishop's palace. The core of the museum, upstairs, is a collection of 18th- and 19th-century paintings donated by Baron Henri-Alexandre Gérard more than a century ago. Notable are an early work by neoclassical master Jacques-Louis David—*Le Philosophe (The Philosopher)*—and *Sapho* by Antoine-Jean Gros, a moonlit version of the Greek poetess' death that influenced Géricault and Delacroix. Don't miss the museum's 19th-century courtroom and its elaborate chapel—gushing with early 17th-century "angels" that look like oversexed cherubs.

Cost and Hours: €7, combo-ticket with other Bayeux museums-€12 or €15, daily May-Sept 9:30-18:30, shorter hours off-season, near the cathedral at 37 Rue du Bienvenu, tel. 02 31 92 14 21, www.bayeuxmuseum.com.

Battle of Normandy Memorial Museum (Musée Mémorial de la Bataille de Normandie)

This museum provides a manageable, if dry, overview of WWII's Battle of Normandy. With its many maps and timelines of the epic battle to liberate northern France, it's aimed at military history buffs. You'll get a good briefing on the Atlantic Wall (the German fortifications stretching along the coast—useful before visiting Longues-sur-Mer), learn why Normandy was selected as the landing site, understand General Charles de Gaulle's contributions to the invasion, and realize the key role played by aviation. You'll also appreciate the challenges faced by doctors, war correspondents, and civil engineers (who had to clean up after the battles—the gargantuan bulldozer on display looks useful).

Cost and Hours: €7, combo-ticket with other Bayeux museums-€12 or €15, daily May-Sept 9:30-18:30, Oct-Dec and mid-Feb-April 10:00-12:30 & 14:00-18:00, closed Jan-mid-Feb, last entry one hour before closing, on Bayeux's ring road, 20 minutes on foot from center on Boulevard Fabian Ware, free parking, tel. 02 31 51 46 90, www.bayeuxmuseum.com.

Film: A 25-minute film gives a good summary of the Normandy invasion from start to finish (shown in English May-Sept at 10:30, 12:00, 14:00, 15:30, and 17:00; Oct-April at 10:30, 14:45, and 16:15).

Nearby: A right out of the museum leads along a footpath to the **Monument to Reporters,** a grassy walkway lined with white roses and stone monuments listing, by year, the names of reporters who have died in the line of duty from 1944 to today. Some years have been kinder to journalists than others. The path continues to the **British Military Cemetery,** decorated with 4,144 simple gravestones marking the final resting places of these fallen soldiers. The memorial's Latin inscription reads, "In 1944, the British came to free the homeland of William the Conqueror." Interestingly, this cemetery has soldiers' graves from all countries involved in the battle of Normandy (even Germany) except the United States, which requires its soldiers to be buried on US property—such as the American Cemetery at Omaha Beach.

Sleeping in Bayeux

I list hotels in every price range here.

NEAR THE TAPESTRY

$$$ Villa Lara**** owns the town's most luxurious accommodations smack in the center of Bayeux. The 28 spacious and well-configured rooms all have brilliant views of the cathedral, and a few have small terraces. Helpful owner Rima and her well-trained staff take excellent care of their guests (Db-€270-360 depending on size and season, palatial Db suite-€420-460, pricey but excellent breakfast-€23, elevator, exercise room, ice machines, comfortable lounges, free and secure parking, between the tapestry museum and TI at 6 Place de Québec, tel. 02 31 92 00 55, www.hotel-villalara.com, info@hotel-villalara.com).

$$$ Hôtel Churchill*,** on a traffic-free street across from the TI, could not be more central. Owners Eric and Patricia are great hosts (ask Eric about his professional soccer career). The hotel has 32 plush-and-pricey rooms with wood furnishings, big beds, and convivial public spaces peppered with historic photos of Bayeux's liberation (small Db-€130, bigger Db-€155, deluxe Db or Tb-€187, Qb-€207, 14 Rue St. Jean, tel. 02 31 21 31 80, www.hotel-churchill.fr, info@hotel-churchill.fr).

$$$ Hôtel le Lion d'Or*,** General Eisenhower's favorite hotel in Bayeux, draws a loyal, American and British clientele who love the historic aspect of staying here. It has well-worn Old World public spaces, 31 oddly stylish rooms, and responsive staff (standard Db-€130-140, bigger Db-€140-175, deep discounts possible off-season—check their website, extra bed-€30, breakfast-€13, no elevator, limited but secure parking-€9/day, 71 Rue St. Jean, tel. 02 31 92 06 90, www.liondor-bayeux.fr, info@liondor-bayeux.fr).

$$ Hôtel Reine Mathilde** is a solid, centrally located value with good service. There are 16 sharp rooms above an easygoing brasserie (Db-€85), and six large rooms with three-star comfort in an annex next door (Db-€125, Tb-€140, Qb-€155, breakfast-€9.50, one block from the TI at 23 Rue Larcher, tel. 02 31 92

08 13, www.hotel-bayeux-reinemathilde.fr, hotel.reinemathilde@orange.fr).

$ Hôtel au Georges VII offers 10 no-star, no-frills rooms (some with only a sink or a shower) with just enough comfort. The rooms are up a tight staircase above a central café, and the bartender doubles as the receptionist (S with shower only-€39, Sb-€42, Db-€48, Tb-€75, Qb-€82, breakfast-€8, 19 Rue St. Martin, tel. 02 31 92 28 53, augeorges7@orange.fr).

CHAMBRES D'HOTES NEAR THE CATHEDRAL

$$$ Le Petit Matin, run by friendly Pascal, is a central and handsome bed-and-breakfast with good public spaces, five stylish rooms with big bathrooms, and a *magnifique* back garden (with play toys) on Place Charles de Gaulle (Db-€100, includes breakfast, 9 Rue des Terres, tel. 02 31 10 09 27, www.lepetitmatin.com, lepetitmatin@hotmail.fr).

$$ Logis les Remparts, run by bubbly Christèle, is a delightful, three-room bed-and-breakfast situated above an atmospheric Calvados cider-tasting shop. The rooms are big, comfortable, and homey—one is a huge, two-room suite (Db-€65-90, Tb-€80-110, cash only for payments under €200, breakfast-€7, a few blocks above the cathedral on the park-like Place Charles de Gaulle at 4 Rue Bourbesneur, tel. 02 31 92 50 40, www.lecornu.fr, info@lecornu.fr).

$$ Manoir Sainte Victoire is a classy, 17th-century building with three dolled-up rooms, each dedicated to a different modern artist. The rooms have small kitchenettes and views of the cathedral (Db-€90, includes breakfast, 32 Rue de la Jurisdiction, tel. 02 31 22 74 69, mobile 06 37 36 90 95, www.manoirsaintevictoire.com, contact@manoirsaintevictoire.com).

NEAR PLACE ST. PATRICE

These hotels just off the big Place St. Patrice are a 10-minute walk up Rue St. Martin from the TI (a 15-minute walk to the tapestry).

$$$ Hôtel d'Argouges*** (dar-goozh) is named for its builder, Lord d'Argouges. This tranquil retreat has a minichâteau feel with classy public spaces, lovely private gardens, and 28 standard-comfort rooms. The hotel is run by formal Madame Ropartz, who has had every aspect of the hotel renovated (Db-€127, larger Db-€149, Tb-€170, fine family suites-€240, deluxe family suite-€290 for up to 6—works fine for two couples, extra bed-€20, breakfast-€14, no elevator, secure free parking, just off Place St. Patrice at 21 Rue St. Patrice, tel. 02 31 92 88 86, www.hotel-dargouges.com, info@hotel-dargouges.com).

$$ B&B Hôtel de Sainte Croix offers three big rooms with cavernous bathrooms in a traditional manor home (Db-€94, Tb-

€135, Qb-€165, cash only, includes good breakfast, 12 Rue du Marché at Place St. Patrice, mobile 06 08 09 62 69, www.hotel-de-sainte-croix.com, contact@hotel-de-sainte-croix.com, friendly Florence).

$$ Hôtel Mogador** is a simple but good 14-room budget value. Choose between wood-beamed rooms on the busy square, or quiet but slightly faded rooms off the street. There are no public areas beyond the small breakfast room and tiny courtyard (Sb-€57, Db-€67, Tb-€78, Qb-€93, breakfast-€9, Wi-Fi, 20 Rue Alain Chartier at Place St. Patrice, tel. 02 31 92 24 58, www.hotelmo.fr, lemogador@gmail.com).

IN THE COUNTRYSIDE NEAR BAYEUX

$$ La Ferme du Pressoir is a lovely, traditional B&B on a big working farm that is immersed in Norman landscapes about 20 minutes south of Bayeux. If you've ever wanted to stay on a real French farm yet rest in cozy comfort, this is the place. The five rooms are filled with wood furnishings and decorated with bright garden themes. Guests share a kitchenette, and larger groups can stay in a cottage with its own kitchen. The experience is vintage Normandy—and so are the kind owners, Jacques and Odile (Db-€90, Tb-€110, Qb-€130, 5 people-€140, discounts for stays of 3 or more nights, includes good breakfast, tel. 02 41 40 71 07, Le Haut St-Louet, just off A-84, exit at Villers-Bocage, get detailed directions from website, www.bandbnormandie.com, lafermedupressoir@bandbnormandie.com).

Eating in Bayeux

Drivers can also consider the short drive to Arromanches for seaside options.

ON OR NEAR RUE ST. JEAN

This traffic-free street is lined with cafés, *crêperies,* and inexpensive dining options.

La Chaumière is the best charcuterie (deli) in town; you'll find salads, quiches, and prepared dishes to go (Tue-Sun open until 19:30, closed for lunch Sun and all day Mon, on Rue St. Jean across from Hôtel Churchill). The grocery store across the street has what you need to complete your picnic.

La Rapière is a lovely, traditional wood-beamed eatery filled with locals enjoying a refined meal and a rare-these-days cheese platter for your finale. The veal with Camembert sauce is memorable. Reservations are wise (€29-52 *menus,* closed for lunch Mon and Wed and all day Sun, 53 Rue St. Jean, tel. 03 31 21 05 45, www.larapiere.net).

NORMANDY

Le Volet Qui Penche is a cool, wine-shop-meets-bistro place run by gentle, English-speaking Pierre-Henri. He serves great *charcuterie* and cheese platters and offers a small selection of à la carte items and wines by the glass but no wine tastings (€10-12 *plat du jour,* salads, *tartines,* nonstop service until 20:00 most days making early dinners easy, closed for lunch Mon and Sat and all day Sun, near the TI at 3 Passage de l'Islet, tel. 03 31 21 98 54).

L'Angle Saint Laurent is a refined and romantic place run by a husband-and-wife team (lovely Caroline speaks English and manages the restaurant, Sébastien cooks). Come here for a special meal of *Normand* specialties done in a contemporary style. The selection is limited, changes often, and is all homemade (€30-40 *menus,* good wine list, closed for lunch Wed and Sat and all day Sun, 2 Rue des Bouchers, tel. 02 31 92 03 01, www.langlesaintlaurent.com).

Le Garde Manger, an easy-going café (attached to the recommended Hôtel Reine Mathilde), offers bistro fare all day (omelets, big salads, pizza) and has a marvelous outside terrace with cathedral views (daily with nonstop service 12:00-22:00, a block from Rue St. Jean at 23 Rue Larcher).

Le Pommier, with street appeal inside and out, is a good place to sample regional products with clever twists in a relaxed yet refined atmosphere. Owner Thierry mixes old and new in his cuisine and decor and focuses on organic food with no GMOs. His fish and meat dishes are satisfying no matter how he prepares them, and there's a vegetarian *menu* as well—a rarity in meat-loving France (two-course *menu* €21, good three-course *menu* from €25, open daily, 38 Rue des Cuisiniers, tel. 02 31 21 52 10, www.restaurantlepommier.com).

Au P'tit Bistrot is a small, casual eatery with a snappy interior and a good reputation for its carefully prepared food. It's warmly run, a nice mix of modern and traditional (€27 *menu,* closed Sun, 31 Rue Larcher, tel. 02 31 92 30 08).

ON PLACE ST. PATRICE

Taverne des Ducs provides big brasserie ambience, efficient and friendly service, comfortable seating inside and out, a full range of choices from *la carte*—including French onion soup, seafood *choucroute* (with sauerkraut), and all the classics—and set *menus.* Try the cooked oysters with garlic sauce, or the *dos de cabillaud à la normande* (cod in butter sauce). They serve until 23:00 (*menus* from €22, open daily, 41 Rue St. Patrice, tel. 02 31 92 09 88).

Bayeux Connections

From Bayeux by Train to: Paris' Gare St. Lazare (9/day, 2.5 hours, some change in Caen), **Amboise** (2/day, 4.5 hours, change in Caen and Tours' St-Pierre-des-Corps), **Rouen** (14/day, 2.5 hours, change in Caen), **Caen** (20/day, 20 minutes), **Honfleur** (2-3/day, 20-minute train to Caen, then 1-hour PrestoBus—line #39—express bus to Honfleur; more with train to Caen and scenic 2-hour ride on bus #20 via the coast; for bus information, call 02 31 89 28 41, www.busverts.fr), **Pontorson/Mont St-Michel** (3/day, 2 hours to Pontorson, then bus to Mont St-Michel; also consider Hôtel Churchill's faster shuttle van—described below).

By Bus to the D-Day Beaches: Bus Verts du Calvados offers minimal service to D-Day beaches with stops in Bayeux at Place St. Patrice and at the train station (schedules at TI, tel. 08 10 21 42 14, www.busverts.fr). Lines #74/#75 run east to Arromanches and Juno Beach (3-5/day, none on Sun Sept-June; 30 minutes to Arromanches, 50 minutes to Juno Beach), and line #70 runs west to the American Cemetery and Vierville-sur-Mer (3/day in summer, 2/day off-season, none on Sun Sept-June, 35 minutes to American Cemetery, 45 minutes to Vierville-sur-Mer). Because of the schedules, you're usually stuck with either too much or too little time at either sight if you try to take the bus round-trip; consider a taxi one way and a bus the other.

By Shuttle Van to Mont St-Michel: Two services run shuttle van day trips to Mont St-Michel (about 1.5 hours each way, plus at least 3 hours at Mont St-Michel): **Hôtel Churchill** (€65/person; available to the public, though hotel clients get a small discount; details at www.hotel-churchill.fr) and **Bayeux Shuttle** (around €55/person, check website for schedules and to sign up, www.bayeuxshuttle.com). Either trip is a terrific deal, as you'll get a free tour of Normandy along the way from your knowledgeable driver.

D-Day Beaches

The 54 miles of Atlantic coast north of Bayeux—stretching from Utah Beach in the west to Sword Beach in the east—are littered with WWII museums, monuments, cemeteries, and battle remains left in tribute to the courage of the British, Canadian, and American armies that successfully carried out the largest military operation in history: D-Day. (It's called *Jour J* in French.) It was on these serene beaches, at the crack of dawn on June 6, 1944, that the Allies finally gained a foothold in France; from this moment, Nazi Europe was destined to crumble.

"The first 24 hours of the invasion will be decisive... The fate of Germany depends on the outcome... For the Allies, as well as Germany, it will be the longest day."
—Field Marshal Erwin Rommel to his aide, April 22, 1944 (from *The Longest Day,* by Cornelius Ryan)

June 6, 2014, marked the 70th anniversary of the landings. It was a huge deal here, given how few D-Day veterans are still alive. Locals talk of the last visits of veterans with heartfelt sorrow; they have adored seeing the old soldiers in their villages and fear losing the firsthand accounts of the battles. All along this rambling coast, locals will never forget what the troops and their families sacrificed all those years ago. A warm regard for Americans has survived political disputes, from de Gaulle to "Freedom Fries." This remains particularly friendly soil for Americans—a place where their soldiers are still honored and the image of the US as a force for good has remained largely untarnished.

PLANNING YOUR TIME

I've listed the D-Day sites from east to west, starting with Arromanches (note that several are closed in January). Many visitors prefer to focus on the American sector (west of Arromanches), rather than the British and Canadian sectors (Arromanches and eastward), which have been overbuilt with resorts, making it harder to envision the events of June 1944. The American sector looks today very much as it would have 70 years ago. For more information on visiting the D-Day beaches, www.normandiememoire.com is a useful resource.

D-Day Sites in One Day

If you have only one day, I'd spend it entirely on the beaches and miss the Caen Memorial Museum. (If you want to squeeze in the museum, visit it on your way to or from the beaches. But remember that the American Cemetery closes at 18:00 mid-April–mid-Sept and at 17:00 the rest of the year—and you need at least 1.5 hours there.) With the exciting sites and museums along the beaches, the Caen Memorial Museum is less important for most.

If you're traveling by car, begin on the cliffs above Arromanches. From there, visit Port Winston and the D-Day Landing Museum, then continue west to Longues-sur-Mer and tour the German gun battery there. Spend your afternoon visiting the American Cemetery and its thought-provoking visitors center, walking on Omaha Beach at Vierville-sur-Mer, and exploring the Pointe du Hoc Ranger Monument. With an extra half-day, spend

D-Day Beaches

To Cherbourg — D-15, D-421 — Utah Beach

English

D-14

•Ste-Mère Eglise

UTAH BEACH LANDING MUSEUM

POINTE DU HOC

Omaha Beach

D-15

N-13, D-913

Banc du Grand Vey

Vierville-sur-Mer — 6

AMERICAN CEMETERY

CHURCH AT ANGOVILLE-AU-PLAIN

D-514

•St-Côme-du-Mont

La Cambe

5

St-Laurent

D-514

Isigny-sur-Mer

GERMAN CEMETERY

Formigny — 7 — **OVERLORD MUSEUM**

N-13

D-903

Carentan

D-113

Vire

D-5

D-971

Taute

D-11

D-5

N-174

D-15

D-10, D-572

D-6

Balleroy

St-Lô — D-972

N O R M

5 Kilometers

5 Miles

N-174

To Mont St-Michel

D-9

❶ La Ferme du Pressoir B&B
❷ Ferme de la Rançonnière & Manoir de Mathan
❸ Le Mas Normand B&B
❹ André & Madeleine Sebire B&B
❺ Hôtel La Sapinière
❻ Hôtel du Casino
❼ Ferme du Mouchel & La Ferme aux Chats

it at the Utah Beach sites (to learn about the paratroopers' role in the invasion), then head off to Mont St-Michel or Honfleur.

Canadians will want to start at the Juno Beach Centre and Canadian Cemetery (in Courseulles-sur-Mer, 10 minutes east of Arromanches).

No Car? You can rent a car for a day, or better, take a mini-van tour or taxi from Bayeux, or—for a really full day—combine a visit to the Caen Memorial Museum with their guided minivan tour of the beaches. Public transport is available, but not practical for more than one sight. Bike riding is dicey as roads are narrow (no bike lanes), there are plenty of blind curves, and traffic is constant.

GETTING AROUND THE D-DAY BEACHES
On Your Own

Though the minivan excursions listed below teach important history lessons—drawing Americans and Canadians out of their cars—**renting a car** is a far less expensive way to visit the beaches, particularly for three or more people.

However, if you're staying in Paris and want to make the

D-Day beaches a day trip in a rental car, think twice. A train from Paris to Caen (the most convenient place to pick up a car) takes over two hours. Then you'll face rental paperwork and at least a half-hour drive to your first stop at Arromanches. Just getting to and from the D-Day beaches will take about six hours out of your day. A better alternative is to book a service that will meet you at a train station and drive you to sights (see "By Taxi" and "By Fully Guided Minivan Tour" next). Or take a bus tour that starts in Paris.

Very limited **bus service** links Bayeux, the coastal town of Arromanches, and the most impressive sites of D-Day.

By Taxi

Taxi minivans shuttle up to seven people between the key sites at reasonable rates (which vary depending on how far you go). Allow €240 for an eight-hour taxi day (€300 on Sun) to visit the top Utah and Omaha Beach sites (with no guiding, of course). Figure about €21 each way between Bayeux and Arromanches, €37 between Bayeux and the American Cemetery, and €100 for a 2.5-hour visit to Omaha Beach sites from Bayeux or Arromanches (50 percent surcharge after 19:00 and on Sun, taxi tel. 02 31 92 92 40 or mobile 06 70 40 07 96, www.taxisbayeux.com, taxisbayeux@orange.fr).

Abbeilles Taxis offer D-Day excursions from Caen (€200/5-hour visit, tel. 02 31 52 17 89, www.taxis-abbeilles-caen.com).

By Fully Guided Minivan Tour

An army of small companies offers all-day excursions to the D-Day beaches from Bayeux or nearby. Demand has grown—as has the guide supply to meet it—and today it seems that anyone with passable English wants to guide. Travelers beware. Anyone can get you around the beaches, but effective teaching of the events is another story. You should expect your guide to deliver coherent history lessons and go with you to all sights (and not orient and disperse you).

The tour companies and guides listed in this section are people I trust to take your time seriously. Most deliver riveting commentary about these moving sites. To land one of these top-notch guides, book your tour in advance (3-6 months is best during peak periods), or pray for a last-minute cancellation. While you can save by hiring a guide who offers half-day tours, a full day on the beaches is right for most. To spend less, look for a guide who will join you in your rental car.

Many tours prefer to pick up in or near Bayeux, and a few levy a small surcharge for a Caen pickup. Many guides skip Arromanches, preferring to focus on sights farther west. While some companies discourage children, others (including Dale Booth, Mathias Leclere, Victory Tours, Sylvain Kast, and Edward Robinson) welcome them.

Cost: These tours are pricey because you're hiring a professional guide and driver/vehicle for the day. All guides charge about the same. A few have regularly scheduled departures available for individual sign-ups (figure on paying about €90/person for a day and €60/person for a half-day). Private groups should expect to pay €500-660 for up to eight people for all day and €250-330 for a half-day. Most tours don't go inside museums (which have good explanations posted in any case), but those that do usually include entry fees—ask. Although many guides offer all-day tours only, these guides may do half-day trips: Bayeux Shuttle, Normandy Sightseeing Tours, Vanessa Letourneur, Edward Robinson, Rodolphe Passera, Victory Tours, and Mathias Leclere.

Working with Your Guide: If hiring a private guide, take charge of your tour if you have specific interests (some guides can get lost in battle minutiae that you don't have time for). Request extra time at the Normandy American Cemetery to see the excellent visitors center.

Scheduled Tours

The following services are designed for individual sign-ups (though all will do private groups as well).

Bayeux Shuttle, run by British expat Andy Sutherland, works hard to incorporate technology (online sign-ups, GPS info displayed onboard) and great guiding into their tours. It's user-friendly for individuals: The pick-up point is in Bayeux, and you can usually book at the last minute. Check www.bayeuxshuttle.com for their latest offers (and other tours); they generally offer half-day tours for about €50 and full-day tours for about €95.

Normandy Sightseeing Tours delivers a French perspective through the voices of its small fleet of well-trained guides and will pick you up anywhere you like—for a price (€45 morning tour, €60 afternoon tour, €90 all-day tour, tel. 02 31 51 70 52, www.normandy-sightseeing-tours.com).

The **Caen Memorial Museum** runs a busy program of half-day tours covering the American and Canadian sectors in combination with a visit to the museum. This option works well for those who have limited time.

Private Tours by Ex-Pats

The following guides offer tours only for private parties. All have their own vehicles; some are happy to ride in your car.

Dale Booth is a fine historian, D-Day author, and riveting storyteller. He leads tours for up to eight people to the American, Canadian, and British sectors (tel. 02 33 71 53 76, www.dboothnormandytours.com, dboothholidays@sfr.fr).

Normandy Battle Tours are led by likable, easygoing Stuart Robertson, who is an effective teacher, D-Day author, and historian. He also owns a bed-and-breakfast near Ste-Mère Eglise and offers combo accommodation/tour packages (tel. 02 33 41 28 34, www.normandybattletours.com, stuart@normandybattletours.com).

D-Day Historian Tours are run by Paul Woodadge, a passionate historian and author who takes your learning seriously. He offers private tours in his minivan of the D-Day beaches and inland battlefields (mobile 07 88 02 76 57, www.ddayhistorian.com, paul@ddayhistorian.com).

D-Day Landing Tours is run by Scottish Eric and French Michelle Le Doux-Turnbull, whose tours cover all sectors—American, British, and Canadian—over one day or a week. Eric enjoys involving his clients in their tour and delivers history with humor and respect (tel. 02 33 30 14 69, www.ddaylandingtours.com, info@ddaylandingtours.com).

Countdown to D-Day

1939 On September 1, Adolf Hitler invades the Free City of Danzig (today's Gdańsk, Poland), sparking World War II.

1940 Germany's "Blitzkrieg" ("lightning war") quickly overwhelms France, Nazis goose-step down Avenue des Champs-Elysées, and the country is divided into Occupied France (the north) and Vichy France (the south, ruled by right-wing French). Just like that, nearly the entire Continent is fascist.

1941 The Allies (Britain, the Soviet Union, and others) peck away at the fringes of "fortress Europe." The Soviets repel Hitler's invasion at Moscow, while the Brits (with American aid) battle German U-boats for control of the seas. On December 7, Japan bombs the US naval base at Pearl Harbor, Hawaii. The US enters the war against Japan and its ally, Germany.

1942 Three crucial battles—at Stalingrad, El-Alamein, and Guadalcanal—weaken the German forces and their ally Japan. The victorious tank battle at El-Alamein in the deserts of North Africa soon gives the Allies a jumping-off point (Tunis) for the first assault on the Continent.

1943 More than 150,000 Americans and Brits, under the command of George Patton and Bernard "Monty" Montgomery, land in Sicily and begin working their way north through Italy. Meanwhile, Germany has to fend off tenacious Soviets on their eastern front.

1944 On June 6, 1944, the Allies launch "Operation Over-lord," better known as D-Day. The Allies amass three million soldiers and six million tons of *matériel* in England in preparation for the biggest fleet-led invasion in history—across the English Channel to France, then eastward toward Berlin. The Germans, hunkered down in northern France, know an invasion is imminent, but the Allies keep the details top secret. On the

Allan Bryson is a student of the Normandy campaign. He provides tours for up to eight people covering the American, British, and Canadian sectors and loves sharing his knowledge (www.firstnormandybattlefieldtours.com, firstnormandy@sfr.fr).

Edward Robinson, who is Irish, informal, and chatty (a national trait?), has previously guided for the Caen Memorial Museum and fires important information at you like a machine gun. Taking up to six passengers in his minivan, he tries to get off the night of June 5, more than 180,000 soldiers board ships and planes, not knowing where they are headed until they're under way. Each one carries a note from General Dwight D. Eisenhower: "The tide has turned. The free men of the world are marching together to victory."

At 6:30 on June 6, 1944, Americans spill out of troop transports into the cold waters off a beach in Normandy, code-named Omaha. The weather is bad, seas are rough, and the prep bombing has failed. The soldiers, many seeing their first action, are dazed, confused, and weighed down by heavy packs. Nazi machine guns pin them against the sea. Slowly, they crawl up the beach on their stomachs. More than a thousand die. They hold on until the next wave of transports arrives.

Americans also see action at Utah Beach, while the British and Canadian troops storm Sword, Juno, and Gold. All day long, Allied confusion does battle with German indecision—the Nazis never really counter-attack, thinking D-Day is just a ruse, not the main invasion. By day's end, the Allies have taken all five beaches along the Normandy coast and soon begin building two completely artificial harbors, code-named "Mulberry," providing ports for the recon-quest of western Europe. The stage is set for a quick and easy end to the war. Right.

1945 Having liberated Paris (August 26, 1944), the Allies' march on Berlin from the west bogs down, hit by poor supply lines, bad weather, and the surprising German counterpunch at the Battle of the Bulge. Fi-nally, in the spring, the Americans and Brits cross the Rhine, Soviet soldiers close in on Berlin, Hitler shoots himself, and—after nearly six long years of war—Europe is free.

beaten track (www.battleofnormandytours.com, edrobinson@battleofnormandytours.com).

Victory Tours is run by friendly Dutchman Roel (pronounced "rule"), who gives private half-day and all-day tours. His tours are informal and entertaining, but sufficiently informative for most (departs from Bayeux only and meets Paris trains, tel. 02 31 51 98 14, www.victorytours.com, victorytours@orange.fr).

Michael Phillips brings a gentle, relaxed personal perspective to his tours (British mobile 0780-246-8599, from France dial 00-44/780-246-8599, www.d-daytours.com).

D-Day Battle Tours are run by WWII-enthusiast Ellwood von Seibold. He drives a WWII Dodge Command Car and explains events as if you were there (tel. 02 33 94 44 13, mobile 06 32 67 49 15, www.ddaybattletours.com, ellwood@ddaybattletours.com).

Private Tours by Locals

These capable French natives give a local perspective to the D-Day landings.

Sylvain Kast is a genuinely nice person with good overall knowledge and many French family connections to the war; he's strong in the American sector and the roles that the Air Force and paratroopers played (mobile 06 17 44 04 46, www.d-day-experience-tours.com, sylvainkast@yahoo.fr).

Vanessa Letourneur is a highly capable and likable person who can guide anywhere in Normandy. She worked at the Caen Memorial Museum and offers top-notch, half-day tours from Bayeux or Caen (mobile 06 98 95 89 45, www.normandypanorama.com).

Mathias Leclere was born four miles from Juno Beach to a family with three centuries of roots in Normandy—he is part of its soil. Mathias is a self-taught historian who leads half-day, full-day, and multiple-day tours in his minivan (www.ddayguidedtours.com).

Rodolphe Passera speaks fluent English and is a serious student of the Normandy invasion. He works as a guide at the D-Day Landing Museum at Utah Beach and has great energy for teaching. He can join your car or drive you in his Lexus SUV (mobile 06 30 55 63 39, leopardbusinesslanguages@gmail.com).

Bertrand Soudrais is a young, flexible, charming, and hard-working guide whose American wife gives him an inside track on Yankee interests (www.executived-daytours.com).

HELPFUL HINTS

Good Booklet: The free *D-Day Normandy: Land of Liberty* booklet gives succinct reviews of area D-Day museums and sites with current opening times. It's available at TIs, but you usually need to ask for it (or you can download it yourself from www.normandiememoire.com).

Food Strategies: The D-Day landing sites are rural, and you won't find a grocery on every corner. Pack ahead if you plan to picnic.

Arromanches

This small town—part of Gold Beach (in the British landing zone)—was ground zero for the D-Day invasion. The Allies decided it would be easier to build their own port than to try to take one from the Nazis. And so, almost overnight, Arromanches sprouted the immense harbor, Port Winston, which gave the Allies a foothold in Normandy, allowing them to begin their victorious push to Berlin and end World War II. The postwar period brought a long decline. Only recently has the population of tiny Arromanches finally returned to its June 5, 1944, numbers. Here you'll find a good museum, an evocative beach and bluff, and a touristy-but-fun little town that offers a pleasant cocktail of war memories, cotton candy, and beachfront trinket shops. Arromanches makes a great home base for touring the D-Day beaches. Sit on the seawall after dark and listen to the waves lick the sand while you contemplate the events that took place here 70 years ago.

Orientation to Arromanches

TOURIST INFORMATION

The service-oriented TI has the *D-Day Normandy* booklet, a free leaflet illustrating the Port Winston harbor, bus schedules, a listing of area hotels and *chambres d'hôtes,* and helpful Mathilde (daily 10:00-12:00 & 14:00-17:00, longer hours in summer—9:30-19:00 in July-Aug, across the parking lot from the D-Day Landing Museum at 2 Avenue Maréchal Joffre, tel. 02 31 22 36 45, www.ot-arromanches.fr). You may find a seasonal branch TI at the parking lot near Arromanches 360.

ARRIVAL IN ARROMANCHES

The bus stop is located at the top of the town across from the post office. The main parking lot by the museum costs €1.50 per hour (free 19:00-9:00). For free parking and less traffic, look for the lot between the small grocery store and Ideale Hôtel Mountbatten as you enter Arromanches.

HELPFUL HINTS

ATM: An ATM is across from the museum parking lot.

Groceries: A little **supermarket** is a long block above the beach, across from Ideale Hôtel Mountbatten.

Taxi: To get an Arromanches-based **taxi,** call mobile 06 66 62 00 99.

WWII Paraphernalia Store: Arromanches Militaria sells all sorts of D-Day relics (daily 10:00-19:00, 11 Boulevard Gilbert Longuet).

Sights in Arromanches

In this section, I've linked Arromanches' D-Day sites with some self-guided commentary.

▲▲▲Port Winston Artificial Harbor

To appreciate the massive undertaking of creating this harbor in a matter of days, you'll view it from two vantage points: from the cliff above and from the town itself. Start on the cliffs, overlooking the site of the impressive WWII harbor.

Getting There: Drive two minutes toward Courseulles-sur-Mer and pay €3 to park in the big, can't-miss-it lot overlooking the sea. Nondrivers—or drivers who'd rather leave their car in Arromanches—can hike 10 minutes up the hill behind the town's D-Day Landing Museum, or take the free white train from the museum to the top of the bluff (runs daily June-Sept, Sat-Sun only Oct-mid-Nov and April-May, none in winter).

❍ Self-Guided Tour: This commentary will lead you around the site.

• *Find the circular concrete viewpoint tower overlooking the town and the beaches and prepare for your briefing. Beyond Arromanches to the left is the American sector, with Omaha Beach and then Utah Beach (notice the sheer cliffs between these two sectors); below and to the right lie the British and Canadian sectors.*

Now get this: Along the beaches below, the Allies arrived in the largest amphibious attack ever, launching the liberation of Western Europe. On D-Day +1—June 7, 1944—17 old ships sailed 100 miles across the English Channel under their own steam to Arromanches. Their crews sank them so that each bow faced the next ship's stern, forming a sea barrier. Then 500 tugboats towed 115 football-field-size cement blocks (called "Phoenixes") across the channel. These were also sunk, creating a four-mile-long breakwater 1.5 miles offshore. Finally, engineers set up seven floating steel "pierheads" with extendable legs; they then linked these to shore with four mile-long floating roads made of concrete pontoons. (You can see a segment of pontoon road in the parking lot behind you, by the statue of the Virgin Mary.) Soldiers placed 115 antiaircraft guns on the Phoenixes and pontoons, protecting a port the size of Dover, England. Within just six days of operation, 54,000 vehicles, 326,000 troops, and 110,000 tons of goods had crossed the English Channel. An Allied toehold in Normandy was secure. Eleven months later, Hitler was dead and the war was over.

▲▲Arromanches 360° Theater

The domed building just off the cliff-top parking lot houses the powerful film *Normandy's 100 Days*. The screens surrounding you show archival footage and photographs of the endeavor to liberate Normandy (works in any language). In addition to honoring the many Allied and German soldiers who died, it gently reminds us that 20,000 French civilians were killed in aerial bombardments. The experience is as loud and slickly produced as anything at the D-Day beaches. It's more emotional and immersive than educational, and for that reason some prefer to see it at the end of their D-Day experience to sum up all they've seen.

Cost and Hours: €5, €20.50 combo-ticket with Caen Memorial Museum is worthwhile if you plan to visit there as well; shows at :10 and :40 past the hour, daily June-Aug 9:40-18:40, April-May and Sept 10:10-18:10, Oct-mid-Nov 10:10-17:40, these are first and last show times, shorter hours off-season, closed most of Jan, tel. 02 31 06 06 45, www.arromanches360.com.

• *Head down to the town's main parking lot (follow signs to* Musée du Débarquement*) and find the round bulkhead on the seawall, near the D-Day Landing Museum entry. Stand facing the sea.*

The **prefab harbor** was created out there by the British. Since it was Churchill's brainchild, it was named Port Winston. Designed to be temporary (it was used for six months), it was supposed to wash out to sea over time—which is exactly what happened with its twin harbor at Omaha Beach (that one lasted only 12 days, thanks to a terrible storm). If the tide is out, you'll see several rusted floats mired on the sand close in—these supported the pontoon roads. If you stare hard enough at the concrete blocks in the sea to the right, you'll see that one still has what's left of an antiaircraft gun platform on it.

On the hill beyond the museum, you'll spot a Sherman tank, one of 50,000 deployed during the landings. Behind the museum (not viewable from here) is another section of a pontoon road, an antiaircraft gun, and a Higgins boat, which was used to ferry 30 soldiers at a time from naval ships to the beaches. If you can, walk down to the beach and wander among the concrete and rusted litter of the battle—and be thankful that all you hear are birds and surf.

▲D-Day Landing Museum (Musée du Débarquement)

The D-Day Landing Museum, facing the harbor, makes a worthwhile 30-45 minute visit and is the only way to get a full appreciation of how the artificial harbor was built. While gazing through windows at the site of this amazing endeavor, you can study helpful models, videos, and photographs illustrating the construction and use of the prefabricated harbor. Screens over the model show a virtual reconstruction of Port Winston. Those blimp-like objects tethered to the port prevented German planes from getting too close (though the German air force had been made largely irrelevant by this time). Ponder the remarkable undertaking that resulted in this harbor being built in just 12 days, while battles raged. The essential 15-minute film (up the stairs behind the cashier) uses British newsreel footage to illustrate the construction of the port; a different video (10 minutes, far end of ground floor) recalls D-Day. Ask for times when each film is shown in English, or wait for the announcement.

Cost and Hours: €8, daily May-Aug 9:00-19:00, Sept 9:00-18:00, Oct-Dec and Feb-April 10:00-12:30 & 13:30-17:00, closed Jan, pick up English flier at door, tel. 02 31 22 34 31, www. arromanches-museum.com.

Sleeping in Arromanches

Arromanches, with its pinwheels and seagulls, has a salty beach-town ambience that makes it a fun overnight stop. Park in the town's main lot at the museum (€1.50/hour, free 19:00-9:00). For evening fun, do what most do and head for the small bar at **Restaurant "Le Pappagall"** (see "Eating in Arromanches"), or, for more of a nightclub scene, have a drink at **Pub Marie Celeste,** around the corner on Rue de la Poste. Drivers should also consider my sleeping recommendations near Omaha Beach.

$$$ Hôtel de la Marine*** has a knock-out location with point-blank views to the artificial harbor site from most of its 33 comfortable rooms (Db-€116, Tb-€165, Qb-€195, bigger family rooms, includes breakfast, elevator, view restaurant, Quai du Canada, tel. 02 31 22 34 19, www.hotel-de-la-marine.fr, hotel.de.la.marine@wanadoo.fr). Ask about their four swankier, similarly priced rooms in the restored Villa Graziella, a few blocks up.

$$ Hôtel d'Arromanches**, which sits on the main pedestrian drag near the TI, is a good value, with nine mostly small, straightforward rooms (some with water views), all up a tight stairway that feels like a tree house. Here you'll find the cheery, recommended Restaurant "Le Pappagall" and English-speaking Luis at the helm (Db-€70-85, newer "deluxe" Db-€90-99, Tb-€96, breakfast-€10, 2 Rue Colonel René Michel, tel. 02 31 22 36 26, www.hoteldarromanches.fr, reservation@hoteldarromanches.fr).

$$ Le Mulberry** is an intimate place with nine simple rooms and a small restaurant. It's a five-minute walk up from the touristy beach, near the town's church, so expect bells to mark the hour until 22:00 (Db-€85-99, Tb-€102-124, breakfast-€9, reception closed 14:00-16:00 and after 19:00, a block below the church at 6 Rue Maurice Lihare, tel. 02 31 22 36 05, www.lemulberry.fr, mail@lemulberry.fr).

\$\$ Ideale Mountbatten Hôtel***, located a long block up from the water, is an eight-room, two-story, motel-esque place with generously sized, stylish, clean, and good-value lodgings, and welcoming owners Sylvie and Laurent. Upstairs rooms have a little view over the sea (Db-€72-99, Tb-€125-135, breakfast-€10, reception closed 14:00-16:00, easy and free parking, short block below the main post office—PTT—at 20 Boulevard Gilbert Longuet, tel. 02 31 22 59 70, www.hotelarromancheslideal.fr, contact@ hotelarromancheslideal.fr).

IN THE COUNTRYSIDE NEAR ARROMANCHES

\$\$ Ferme de la Rançonnière is a 35-room, country-classy oasis buried in farmland with easy car access to Bayeux and Arromanches (within 15 minutes of each). It's flawlessly maintained, from its wood-beamed, stone-walled rooms to its traditional restaurant (good *menus* from €30) and fireplace-cozy lounge/bar (small Db-€70-100, bigger Db-€110-170, Db suites-€180-215, breakfast-€13, bike rental, service-oriented staff, 4.5 miles southeast from Arromanches in Crépon, tel. 02 31 22 21 73, www.ranconniere.fr, ranconniere@wanadoo.fr).

The same family has two other properties nearby: The **Manoir de Mathan** has 21 similarly traditional but bigger rooms a few blocks away in the same village (comparable prices to main building). An eight-minute drive away, in the village of Asnelles, are seven slick, glassy, modern seaside **apartments** right along the beachfront promenade (€85-180 depending on size, www.gites-en-normandie.eu). For any of these, check in at the main hotel. Book direct so that they can help you choose the property and room that works best for you.

\$\$ Le Mas Normand, 10 minutes east of Arromanches in Ver-sur-Mer, is the child of *Provençale* Mylène and *Normand* Christian. Here you get a warm welcome and the best of both worlds: three lovingly decorated, Provence-style rooms wrapped in 18th-century Norman stone. The place is family-friendly with ample grass, a dog, some chickens, and no smoking (Db-€80-100, Tb-€135, Qb-€155; ask about their fun, funky and tight *roulotte*—a Gypsy-style trailer; includes breakfast; drive to the east end of little Ver-sur-Mer, turn right at Hôtel P'tit Bouchon, take another right where the road makes a "T," and find the sign at 8 Impasse de la Rivière; tel. 02 31 21 97 75, www.lemasnormand.com, lemasnormand@wanadoo.fr).

\$ At André and Madeleine Sebire's B&B, you'll experience a real Norman farm. The hardworking owners offer four modest, homey, and dirt-cheap rooms in the middle of nowhere (Sb-€35, Db-€40, Tb-€45, includes breakfast, 2 miles from Arromanches in the tiny village of Ryes at Ferme du Clos Neuf, tel. 02 31 22 32 34, emmanuelle.sebire@wanadoo.fr, little English spoken). Try these directions: Follow signs into Ryes, then go down the street (Rue de la Forge) that's kitty-corner from the village's lone restaurant. You'll cross a tiny bridge, turn right onto Rue de la Tringale, and follow it for a half-mile until you see a small sign on the right to *Le Clos Neuf.* Park near the tractors.

Eating in Arromanches

You'll find cafés, *crêperies*, and shops selling sandwiches to go (ideal for beachfront picnics). The following restaurants are reliable.

Le Mulberry is a good place to dine on homemade recipes at reasonable prices (*menus* from €20, daily, see hotel listing earlier).

Restaurant "Le Pappagall" (French slang for "parakeet") has tasty mussels, filling fish *choucroute*, "*les* feesh and cheeps," salads, and a full offering with fair prices (daily in high season, closed Wed and possibly other days off-season, see Hôtel d'Arromanches listing, earlier).

Hôtel de la Marine allows you to dine or drink in style on the water (*menus* from €19, cool bar with same views, daily, see hotel listing earlier).

Arromanches Connections

From Arromanches by Bus to: Bayeux (bus #74/#75, 3-5/day, none on Sun Sept-June, 30 minutes); **Juno Beach** (bus #74/#75, 20 minutes). The bus stop is near the main post office, four long blocks above the sea (the stop for Bayeux is on the sea side of the street; the stop for Juno Beach is on the post office side).

American D-Day Sites

The American sector, stretching west of Arromanches, is divided between Omaha and Utah beaches. Omaha Beach starts just a few miles west of Arromanches and has the most important sites for visitors, including the American Cemetery and—just beyond the beach—Pointe du Hoc. Utah Beach sites are farther away (on the road to Cherbourg), but these were also critical to the ultimate success of the Normandy invasion. The American Airborne sector covers a broad area behind Utah Beach and centers on Ste-Mère Eglise. You'll see memorials sprouting up all around the countryside.

Omaha Beach

Omaha Beach is the landing zone most familiar to Americans. This well-defended stretch was where US troops saw their biggest losses (dramatized in the movie S*aving Private Ryan*). I've listed several stops going west from Arromanches.

NORMANDY

▲Longues-sur-Mer Gun Battery

Four German casemates (three with guns intact)—built to guard against seaborne attacks—hunker down at the end of a country road. The guns, 300 yards inland, were arranged in a semicircle to maximize the firing range east and west, and are the only original coastal artillery guns remaining in place in the D-Day region. (Much was scrapped after the war, long before people thought of tourism.) This battery, staffed by 194 German soldiers, was more defended than the better-known Pointe du Hoc (described later). The Longues-sur-Mer Battery was a critical link in Hitler's Atlantic Wall defense, which consisted of more than 15,000 structures stretching from Norway to the Pyrenees. The guns could hit targets up to 12 miles away with relatively sharp accuracy if linked to good target information. The Allies had to take them out.

Cost and Hours: Free and always open; on-site TI open April-Oct daily 10:00-13:00 & 14:00-18:00. The TI's €5.70 booklet is helpful, but skip the €5 tour.

Getting There: You'll find the guns 10 minutes west of Arromanches on D-514. Follow *Port en Bessin* signs; once in Longues-sur-Mer, follow *Batterie* signs; turn right at the town's only traffic light.

Visiting the Battery: Enter the third bunker you pass. It took seven soldiers to manage each gun, which could be loaded and fired six times per minute (the shells weighed 40 pounds). Outside, climb above the bunker and find the hooks that were used to secure camouflage netting, making it nigh-impossible for bombers to locate them.

Head down the path between the second and third bunkers until you reach a lone observation bunker (look for the low-lying concrete roof just before the cliffs). This was designed to direct the firing; field telephones connected the bunker to the gun batteries by underground wires. Walk to the observation bunker to appreciate the strategic view over the Channel. From here you can walk along the glorious *Sentier du Littoral* (coastal path) above the cliffs and see Arromanches in the distance, then walk the road back to your car. You can also drive five minutes down to the water on the small road past the site's parking lot.

The WWI Russian cannon near the parking lot's info kiosk looks like a Tinkertoy compared to those up the short trail.

NORMANDY

▲▲▲WWII Normandy American Cemetery and Memorial

"Soldiers' graves are the greatest preachers of peace."
—Albert Schweitzer

Crowning a bluff just above Omaha Beach and the eye of the D-Day storm, 9,387 brilliant white-marble crosses and Stars of David glow in memory of Americans who gave their lives to free Europe on the beaches below. You'll want to spend at least 1.5 hours at this stirring site.

Cost and Hours: Free, daily mid-April-mid-Sept   9:00-18:00, mid-Sept-mid-April 9:00-17:00, tel. 02 31 51 62 00, www.abmc.gov. Park carefully, as break-ins are a problem. You'll find good WCs and water fountains at the parking lot. Guided 45-minute tours are offered a few times a day in high season (usually at 11:00 and 14:00—call ahead to confirm times).

Getting There: The cemetery is just east of St-Laurent-sur-Mer and northwest of Bayeux in Colleville-sur-Mer. From route D-514, you'll enter the village of Colleville-sur-Mer; at the big roundabout (overlooked by the Overlord Museum, described later), you can't miss the signs to the cemetery.

Visiting the Cemetery: Your visit begins at the impressive **visitors center.** Pass security, pick up the handout, sign the register, and allow time to appreciate the superb displays. On the arrival floor, computer terminals provide access to a database containing the story of each US serviceman who died in Normandy.

Descend one level, where you'll learn about the invasion preparations and the immense logistical challenges they presented. The heart of the center tells the stories of the brave individuals who gave their lives to liberate people they could not know, and shows the few possessions they died with (about 25,000 Americans died in the battle for Normandy). This adds a personal touch to the D-Day landings and prepares visitors for the fields of white crosses and Stars of David outside. The pressure on these men to succeed in this battle is palpable. There are a manageable number of display cases, a few moving videos (including an interview with Dwight Eisenhower), and a touching 16-minute film with excerpts of letters home from servicemen who now lie at rest in this cemetery (cushy theater chairs, on the half-hour, you can enter late).

A lineup of informational plaques provides a worthwhile and

succinct overview of key events from September 1939 to June 5, 1944. Starting with June 6, 1944, the plaques present the progress of the landings in three-hour increments. Amazingly, Omaha Beach was secured within six hours of the landings.

You'll exit the visitors center through the "Sacrifice Gallery," with photos and bios of several people now buried here, as well as some survivors. A voice reads the names of each of the cemetery's permanent residents on a continuous loop.

A path from the visitors center leads to a bluff overlooking the piece of Normandy **beach** called "that embattled shore—portal of freedom." It's quiet and peaceful today, but the horrific carnage of June 6, 1944, is hard to forget. An orientation table looks over the sea. Nearby, steps climb down to the beautiful beach below. A walk on the beach is a powerful experience and a must if you are *sans* both car and tour (visitors with cars can easily drive to the beach at Vierville-sur-Mer).

In the **cemetery,** you'll find a striking memorial with a soaring statue representing the spirit of American youth. Around the statue, giant reliefs of the Battle of Normandy and the Battle of Europe are etched on the walls. Behind is the semicircular Garden of the Missing, with the names of 1,557 soldiers who were never found. A small metal button next to the name indicates one whose body was eventually found—there aren't many.

Finally, wander through the peaceful and poignant sea of headstones. Notice the names, home states, and dates of death (but no birth dates) inscribed on each. Dog-tag numbers are etched into the lower backs of the crosses. During the campaign, the dead were buried in temporary cemeteries throughout various parts of Normandy. After the war, the families of the soldiers could decide whether their loved ones  should remain with their comrades or be brought home (61 percent opted for repatriation).

A disproportionate number of officers are buried here, including General Theodore Roosevelt, Jr., who insisted on joining the invasion despite having a weak heart—he died from a heart attack one month after D-Day (Ted's grave—and his brother Quentin's—lie along the sea, about 150 yards down, in the back-right corner of the second grouping of graves, just after the row 27 marker—look for the gold lettering). Families knew that these officers would want to be buried alongside the men with whom they fought. Also buried here are two of the Niland brothers, now famous from *Sav-

ing Private Ryan (in the middle of the cemetery, just before the circular chapel, turn right down row 15—the row marked by the letter "F"; theirs are the ninth and tenth crosses down).

France has given the US permanent free use of this 172-acre site. It is immaculately maintained by the American Battle Monuments Commission.

▲▲Omaha Beach/Vierville-Sur-Mer

This essential detour for drivers allows direct access onto Omaha Beach. From the American Cemetery, drive west along D-514, into St-Laurent, then take a one-way loop drive along the beach, following *Vierville s/Mer par la Côte* signs on D-517. As you drop down toward the beach, WWII junkies should at least stop at the parking lot of the **Omaha Beach Museum (Musée Memorial d'Omaha Beach).** Outside the museum, you'll see a rusted metal object with several legs, called a "Czech hedgehog"—thousands of these were placed on the beaches by the Germans to foil the Allies' advance. Find the American 155mm "Long Tom" gun nearby, and keep this image in mind for your stop at Pointe du Hoc (this artillery piece is similar in size to the German guns that were targeted by US Army Rangers at that site). The Sherman tank is one of the best examples of the type that attacked the D-Day beaches. The museum itself is skippable (€6.50, daily July-Aug 9:30-19:30, June until 19:00, April-May and Sept until 18:30, shorter hours off-season, closed mid-Nov-mid-Feb, tel. 02 31 21 97 44, www.musee-memorial-omaha.com, good 25-minute film).

Continuing past the Omaha Beach Museum, you'll reach a big roundabout just above the water. To **access the beach,** take the second exit, which leads you along the beachfront road and through the village of Le Ruquet. Drive about one mile (1.5 kilometers)—passing Hôtel La Sapinière's airy and reasonable café; handy and good if you're ready for a meal—to where the road ends. This is a good place to get out of your car to appreciate the challenges that American soldiers faced on D-Day.

The small German bunker and embedded gun protected this point, which offered the easiest access inland from Omaha Beach. It was here that the Americans would establish their first road inland. Find your way out to the beach and stroll to the right to better understand the assignment that American forces were handed on June 6.

Back in your car, retrace your route along the beach (look for worthwhile information boards

On Omaha Beach

Actually walking on Omaha Beach is a powerful ▲▲▲ experience for history buffs—whether you drive there via Vierville-sur-Mer or hike down from the American Cemetery. Let the modern world melt away here and put yourself in those soldiers' combat boots:

You're wasted from a lack of sleep and nervous anticipation. Now you get seasick too, as you're about to land in a small, flat-bottomed boat, cheek-to-jowl with 29 other soldiers. Your water-soaked pack feels like a boulder, and your gun feels even heavier. The boat's front ramp drops open, and you run for your life for 500 yards through water and sand onto this open beach, dodging bullets from above (the landings had to occur at low tide so that mines would be visible).

Omaha Beach witnessed by far the most intense battles of any along the D-Day beaches—although the war planners thought Utah Beach would be more deadly. The hills above were heavily fortified with machine gun and mortar nests. (The aerial, naval, and supporting rocket fire that the Allies poured onto the German defenses failed to put them out of commission.) A single German machine gun could fire 1,200 rounds a minute. That's right—1,200. It's amazing that anyone survived. The highest casualty rates in Normandy occurred here at Omaha Beach, nicknamed "Bloody Omaha." Though there are no accurate figures for D-Day, it is estimated that on the first day of the campaign, the Allies suffered 10,500 casualties (killed, wounded, and missing)—6,000 of whom were Americans. Estimates for Omaha Beach casualties range from 2,500 to 4,800 killed and wounded on that day, many of whom drowned after being wounded. But thanks to an overwhelming effort and huge support from the US and Royal navies, 34,000 Americans would land on the beach by day's end.

If the tide's out, you'll notice some remains of rusted metal objects. Omaha Beach was littered with obstacles to disrupt the landings. Thousands of metal poles and Czech hedgehogs, miles of barbed wire, and more than six million mines were scattered along these beaches. At least 150,000 tons of metal were taken from the beaches after World War II, and they still didn't get it all. They never will.

along the sea) and hug the coast past the flags heading toward the Pointe de la Percée cliff, which, from here, looks very Pointe du Hoc-like (American Army Rangers mistook this cliff for Pointe du Hoc, costing them time and lives). A local artist made that striking **metal sculpture** rising from the waves in honor of the liberating forces, and to symbolize the rise of freedom on the wings of hope.

Keep hugging the coastline on D-517 and pull over near the Hôtel Casino to explore the **two German bunkers** just below the hotel—one now transformed into a monument to US National

Guard troops who landed on D-Day. Antitank guns housed in these bunkers were not aimed out to sea, but instead were positioned to fire directly up the beach.

Look out to the ocean. It was here that the Americans assembled their own floating bridge and artificial harbor (à la Arromanches). The harbor functioned for 12 days before being destroyed by an unusually vicious June storm (the artificial port at Arromanches and a makeshift port at Utah Beach were used until November of 1944). Have a seaside drink or lunch at the hotel's view café, and contemplate a stroll toward the jutting Pointe de la Percée.

Drive uphill past Hôtel Casino on D-517. Look to your left to find two small concrete window frames high in the cliff that served as German machine gun nests, then notice the pontoon bridge on the right that had been installed at this beach. After the storm, it was moved to Arromanches and used as a second off-loading ramp. It was discovered only a few years ago...in a junkyard.

At the junction with D-514, turn right (west) toward Pointe du Hoc. Along the way, near the far end of the hamlet of Englesqueville la Percée, you'll see a 10th-century fortified farm on the left offering **Calvados tastings.** To try some, cross the drawbridge, ring the rope bell, and meet charming owners Soizic and Bernard Lebrec. Start with their cider, move on to Pommeau (a mix of apple juice and Calvados), and finish with Calvados. They also sell various other regional products, including D-Day Honey, which is made by one of the guides I recommend (tel. 09 60 38 60 17, mobile 06 76 37 46 41). Ask to see the farm's own D-Day monument; erected in September 1944, it's likely one of the earliest in France.

▲▲▲Pointe du Hoc

The intense bombing of the beaches by Allied forces is best imagined here, where US Army Rangers scaled impossibly steep cliffs to disable a German gun battery. Pointe du Hoc's bomb-cratered, lunar-like landscape and remaining bunkers make it one of the most evocative of the D-Day sites.

Cost and Hours: Pointe du Hoc is free and open daily mid-April-mid Sept 9:00-18:00, off-season 9:00-17:00, tel. 02 31 51 62 00.

Getting There: It's off route D-514, 20 minutes west of the American Cemetery.

Visiting Pointe du Hoc: Park near the visitors center, where you can get a concise overview of the heroic efforts to take the Pointe. Relax in the cinema for an eight-minute film that offers first-person accounts of this Mission Impossible assault. Then follow the path toward the sea.

Upon entering the site, you'll see an **opening** on your left that's as wide as a manhole cover and about six feet deep. This was a machine gun nest. Three soldiers would be holed up down there—a commander, a gun loader, and the gunner.

Climb to the **viewing platform** ahead and survey the scene. This point of land was the Germans' most heavily fortified position along the D-Day beaches. It held six 155mm guns that were capable of firing up to 13 miles. The farthest part of Omaha Beach is 9 miles to the east; Utah Beach is only 8 miles to the west. For the American landings to succeed, the Allies had to run the Germans off this cliff. So they bombed it to smithereens, dropping over 1,500 tons of bombs on this one cliff top. That explains the craters. Heavy bombing started in April 1944, continued into May, and hit its peak on June 6—making this the most intensely bombarded site of the D-Day targets. Even so, only about 5 percent of the bunkers were destroyed. The problem? Multiple direct hits were needed to destroy bunkers like these, which were well-camouflaged, and whose thick, dense walls were heavily reinforced.

Walk around. The battle-scarred **German bunkers** and the cratered landscape remain much as the Rangers left them. You can crawl in and out of the bunkers at your own risk, but picnicking is forbidden—the bunkers are considered gravesites. Notice the six large, round open sites with short rusted poles stuck in a concrete center. Each held a gun (picture the 155mm gun you saw by the Omaha Beach Museum). Destroying these was the Rangers' goal.

Walk to the bunker hanging over the ocean with the stone column at its top. This **memorial** symbolizes the Ranger "Dagger," planted firmly in the ground. Read the inscription, then walk below the sculpture to peer into the narrow slit of the bunker. From here, men would direct the firing of the six anti-ship guns via telephone.

Look over the cliff, and think about the 205 handpicked Rangers who attempted a castle-style assault. They landed to your right, using rocket-propelled grappling hooks connected to 150-foot ropes, and climbed ladders borrowed from London fire departments. With the help of supporting naval fire, the Rangers would take relatively light casualties in the initial attack, partially because the Germans weren't prepared. They regarded their position as nearly impregnable to any attack from the sea.

Timing was critical, though; the Rangers had just 30 minutes before the rising tide would overcome the men below. After finally succeeding in their task, the Rangers found that the guns had been moved—the Germans had put telegraph poles in their place. (Commander Erwin Rommel had directed that all coastal guns not under the cover of roofs be pulled back due to air strikes.) The Rangers eventually found the guns stashed a half-mile inland and destroyed them.

▲German Military Cemetery

To ponder German losses, visit this somber, thought-provoking resting place of 21,000 German soldiers. This was originally the site for one of 15 temporary American cemeteries in Normandy. Compared to the American Cemetery at St. Laurent, this site is more about humility than hero worship. It's appropriately bleak, with two graves per simple marker (dark and lying flat against the ground instead of white crosses) and dark, basalt crosses in groups of five scattered about. Birth and death dates (day/month/year) on the graves make clear the tragedy of the soldiers' short lives. The circular mound in the middle covers the remains of 207 unknown soldiers and 89 others. Notice the ages of the young soldiers who gave their lives for a cause they couldn't understand. In the parking lot, a small visitors center gives more information on this and other German war cemeteries.

Cost and Hours: Free, daily April-Oct 8:00-19:00, off-season generally 9:00-17:00, tel. 02 31 22 70 76.

Getting There: It's on A-84 in the village of La Cambe, 15 minutes south of Pointe du Hoc and 15 minutes west of Bayeux (follow signs reading *Cimetière Militaire Allemand*). To get there from Pointe du Hoc, follow D-514 west, then turn off in Grand-camp for La Cambe and Bayeux (D-199). After crossing over the autoroute, turn left and follow the country roads to the cemetery.

Sleeping near Omaha Beach

With a car, you can find better deals on accommodations and wake up a stone's throw from many landing sites. Besides these recommended spots, you'll pass scads of good-value *chambres d'hôtes* as you prowl the D-Day beaches. The last two places are a few minutes toward Bayeux in the village of Formigny.

$$ Hôtel la Sapinière** is a find just a few steps from the beach at Vierville-sur-Mer. A grassy, beach-bungalow kind of place, it has 15 sharp, crisp rooms, all with private patios, and a lighthearted, good-value restaurant/bar serving €13 omelets and salads, and €16 *plats* (Db-€90, loft Db-€105, Tb/Qb-€130; breakfast-€12, in Le Ruquet in St-Laurent-sur-Mer—10 minutes west of the American Cemetery, take D-517 down to the beach, turn right and keep going; tel. 02 31 92 71 72, www.la-sapiniere.fr, sci-thierry@wanadoo.fr).

$$ Hôtel du Casino** is a good place to experience Omaha Beach. This average-looking hotel has surprisingly comfortable and stylish rooms and sits alone, overlooking the beach in Vierville-sur-Mer, between the American Cemetery and Pointe du Hoc. All rooms have views, but the best face the sea: Ask introverted owner Madame Clémençon for *côté mer* (Db-€100, view Db-€130, extra bed-€16, breakfast-€10, view restaurant with *menus* from €28, café/bar on the beach below, tel. 02 31 22 41 02, hotel-du-casino@ orange.fr). Don't confuse this with Hôtel du Casino in St-Valery-en-Caux.

$$ At **Ferme du Mouchel,** animated Odile rents four colorful and good rooms with sweet gardens in a lovely farm setting in the village of Formigny (Db-€70, Tb-€75-90, Qb-€95-110, cash only, includes breakfast, tel. 02 31 22 53 79, mobile 06 15 37 50 20, www.ferme-du-mouchel.com, odile.lenourichel@orange.fr). Follow the sign from the main road, then turn left down the tree-lined lane when you see the *Le Mouchel* sign.

$$ La Ferme aux Chats, across from the church in the center of Formigny, has welcoming owners, a cozy lounge with a library of D-Day information, and four clean, comfortable, modern rooms at fair prices. Explore the sprawling gardens out back, with chickens, ducks, fish...and nine of those namesake cats (Db-€80, Tb-€95, includes breakfast, tel. 02 31 51 00 88, www.lafermeauxchats.fr, info@fermeauxchats.fr).

Utah Beach

Utah Beach, added late in the planning for D-Day, proved critical. This was where two US paratrooper units (the 82nd and the 101st Airborne Divisions) dropped behind enemy lines the night before the invasion, as dramatized in *Band of Brothers* and *The Longest Day.* Many landed off-target (such as in Ste-Mère Eglise). It was essential for the invading forces to succeed here, then push up the peninsula (which had been intentionally flooded by the Nazis) to the port city of Cherbourg. While the brutality on this beach paled in comparison with the carnage on Omaha Beach, many of the paratroopers missed their targets—causing confusion and worse—and the units that landed here faced a three-week battle before finally taking Cherbourg.

These sights are listed in logical order coming from Bayeux or Omaha Beach. For the first two sights, take the Utah Beach exit (D-913) from N-13 and turn right. Serious sightseers can bundle the Utah Beach Landing Museum, the Airborne Museum in Ste-Mère Eglise, and the "Open Sky Museum" GPS driving tour in one combo-ticket (€15, sold only at Ste-Mère Eglise TI).

Church at Angoville-au-Plain

Just five minutes from the N-13 exit, at this simple Romanesque church, two American medics—Kenneth Moore and Robert Wright—treated German and American wounded while battles raged only steps away. On June 6, American paratroopers landed around Angoville-au-Plain, a few miles inland of Utah Beach, and met fierce resistance from German forces. The two medics set up shop in the small church, and treated American and German soldiers for 72 hours straight, saving many lives. German patrols entered the church on a few occasions. The medics insisted that the soldiers leave their guns outside or leave the church—incredibly, they did. In an amazing coincidence, this 12th-century church is dedicated to two martyrs who were doctors as well.

A faded informational display outside the church recounts the events here; an English handout is available inside. Pass through the small cemetery and enter the church. Inside, several wooden pews toward the rear still have visible bloodstains. Find the new window that honors the American medics and another that honors the paratroopers (€3 requested donation for brochure, daily 9:00-18:00, 2 minutes off D-913 toward Utah Beach).

▲▲▲Utah Beach Landing Museum (Musée du Débarquement)

This is the best museum located on the D-Day beaches, and worth the 45-minute drive from Bayeux. For the Allied landings to succeed, many coordinated tasks had to be accomplished: Paratroopers had to be dropped inland, the resistance had to disable bridges and cut communications, bombers had to deliver payloads on target and on time, the infantry had to land safely on the beaches, and supplies had to follow the infantry closely. This thorough yet manageable museum pieces those many parts together in a series of fascinating exhibits and displays.

Cost and Hours: €8, daily June-Sept 9:30-19:00, Oct-Nov and Jan-May 10:00-18:00, closed Dec, last entry one hour before closing, tel. 02 33 71 53 35, www.utah-beach.com. Guided museum tours are offered (2/day), call ahead for times or ask when you arrive (tours are free, tips appropriate).

Getting There: From Bayeux, travel west toward Cherbourg on N-13 and take the Utah Beach exit (D-913). Turn right at the exit to reach the museum. An American and French flag duo leads to the entry as you approach. You'll park in the "obligitaire" lot, then walk the remaining five minutes.

The road leaving the museum, the Route de la Liberté, runs all the way from Utah Beach to Cherbourg, and in the other direction, on to Paris and Berlin, with every kilometer identified with historic road markers. A mile or so before the museum, watch for the relatively new monument with a quote from Richard Winters, the leader of Easy Company in Stephen Ambrose's WWII classic *Band of Brothers,* that helps even pacifists feel good about what happened here: "Wars do not make men great, but they do bring out the greatness in good men."

Visiting the Museum: Built around the remains of a concrete

German bunker, the museum nestles in the sand dunes on Utah Beach, with floors above and below sea level. Your visit starts with background about the American landings on Utah Beach (20,000 troops landed on the first day alone) and the German defense strategy (Rommel was displeased at what he found two weeks before the invasion). See the outstanding 12-minute film, *Victory in the Sand*, which sets the stage well.

The highlight of the museum is the display of innovative invasion equipment with videos demonstrating how it worked: the remote-controlled Goliath mine, the LVT-2 Water Buffalo and Duck amphibious vehicles, the wooden Higgins landing craft (named for the New Orleans man who invented it), and the best—a fully restored B-26 bomber with its zebra stripes and 11 menacing machine guns, without which the landings would not have been possible (the yellow bomb icons indicate the number of missions a pilot had flown). Enter the simulated briefing room and sense the pilots' nervous energy—would your plane fly *LOW* or *HIGH?* Listen to the many videos as veterans describe how they took the beach and rushed into the interior—including testimony from Easy Company's Richard Winters.

Head upstairs for the stunning grand finale: the large, glassed-in room overlooking the beach. From here, you'll peer over re-created German trenches and feel what it must have felt like to be behind enemy lines. Many German bunkers remain buried in the dunes today. Outside, find the beach access where Americans first broke through Hitler's Atlantic Wall. You can hike up to the small bluff, which is lined with a variety of monuments to the branches of military service that participated in the fight.

To reach the next sight, follow the coastal route (D-421) and signs to Ste-Mère Eglise.

▲Ste-Mère Eglise

This celebrated village lies 15 minutes north of Utah Beach and was the first village to be liberated by the Americans, due largely to its strategic location on the Cotentin Peninsula. The area around Ste-Mère Eglise was the center of action for American paratroopers, whose objective was to land behind enemy lines in support of the American landing at Utah Beach.

For *The Longest Day* movie buffs, Ste-Mère Eglise is a necessary pilgrimage. It was around this village that many paratroopers, facing terrible weather and heavy antiaircraft fire, landed off-target—and many landed in the town. One American paratrooper dangled from the town's church steeple for two hours (a parachute has been reinstalled on the steeple where Private John Steele's became snagged—though not in the correct corner). And though many paratroopers were killed in the first hours of the invasion, the Americans eventually overcame their poor start and managed to take the town (Steele survived his ordeal and the war). They played a critical role in the success of the Utah Beach landings by securing roads and bridges behind enemy lines. Today, the village greets travelers with flag-draped streets and a handful of worthwhile sights.

Drive right to the church and park in the handy €2 lot (or find free parking on side streets). The **TI** on the square across from the church has loads of information and rents audiovisual guides with GPS, allowing you to discover the town and D-Day sites in the area on your own. It's called the **Open Sky Museum**—but actually it's a three-hour driving tour of the region linking all the D-Day sites together (€8, €250 deposit for GPS unit). The TI may sell a combo-ticket good for the Utah Beach Landing Museum, the Airborne Museum, and the Open Sky Museum driving tour (€15, only available at the TI; open July-Aug Mon-Sat 9:00-18:30, Sun 10:00-16:00; Sept and April-June Mon-Sat 9:00-13:00 & 14:00-18:00, Sun 10:00-13:00; shorter hours Oct-March; 6 Rue Eisenhower, tel. 02 33 21 00 33, www.sainte-mere-eglise.info).

Town Church

At the center of town, the 700-year-old medieval church on the town square was the focus of the action during the invasion. It now holds two contemporary stained-glass windows that acknowledge the heroism of the Allies. The window in the left transept features St. Michael, patron saint of paratroopers.

▲Airborne Museum

Housed in two parachute-shaped structures and one low-slung, hanger-like structure, its collection is dedicated to the daring aerial landings that were essential to the success of D-Day. During the invasion, in the Utah Beach sector alone, 23,000 men were dropped from planes (remarkably, only 197 died), along with 1,700 vehicles and 1,800 tons of supplies.

Cost and Hours: €8, daily May-Aug 9:00-19:00, April and Sept 9:30-18:30, shorter hours off-season and closed Jan, 14 Rue Eisenhower, tel. 02 33 41 41 35, www.airborne-museum.org.

Visiting the Museum: In the first building (marked *Planeur Waco*), you'll see a **Waco glider** (104 were flown into Normandy at first light on D-Day) that was used to land supplies in fields to support the paratroopers. Each glider could be used only once. Feel the canvas fuselage and check out the bare-bones interior. The second, larger building holds a **Douglas C-47** plane that dropped parachutists, along with many other supplies essential to the successful landings. Here you'll find mannequins of soldiers with their uniforms, displays of their personal possessions and weapons, and two movies: One focuses on the airborne invasion, and the other venerates President Ronald Reagan's 1984 trip to Normandy. Climb to the view platform to appreciate the wingspan of a C-47. A third structure (labeled *Operation Neptune*) puts you into the paratrooper's experience starting with a night flight and jump, then tracks your progress on the ground past enemy fire using elaborate models and sound effects.

Canadian D-Day Sites

The Canadians' assignment for the Normandy invasions was to work with British forces to take the city of Caen. They hoped to make quick work of Caen, then move on. That didn't happen. The Germans poured most of their reserves, including tanks, into the city and fought ferociously for two months. The Allies didn't occupy Caen until August 1944.

Juno Beach Centre

Located on the beachfront in the Canadian sector, this facility is dedicated to teaching travelers about the vital role Canadian forces played in the invasion, and about Canada in general. (Canada declared war on Germany two years before the United States, a fact little recognized by most Americans today.) After attending the 50th anniversary of the D-Day landings, Canadian veterans were saddened by the absence of information on their contribution (after the US and Britain, Canada contributed the largest number of troops—14,000), so they generated funds to build this place (plaques in front honor key donors).

Cost and Hours: €7, €11 with guided tour of Juno Beach—highly recommended, daily April-Sept 9:30-19:00, Oct and March 10:00-18:00, Nov-Dec and Feb 10:00-17:00, closed Jan, tel. 02 31 37 32 17, www.junobeach.org.

Tours: The best way to appreciate this sector of the D-Day beaches is to take a tour with one of the Centre's capable Canadian guides. The tour covers important aspects of the battles, takes you down into two bunkers and a tunnel of the German defense network, and touches on the changes to the sand dunes and beaches since the war (€5.50 for tour alone, €11 with admission, 45 minutes; April-Oct generally at 10:30 and 14:30, July-Aug also at 11:30 and 16:30; verify times prior to your visit).

Getting There: It's in Courseulles-sur-Mer, about 15 minutes east of Arromanches off D-514. Approaching from Arromanches, as you enter the village of Grave-sur-Mer, watch for the easy-to-miss *Juno Beach-Mémorial* sign marking the turnoff on the left;

you'll drive the length of a sandy spit (passing a marina) to the end of the road, where you'll find the parking lot.

Visiting Juno Beach: Your visit includes many thoughtful exhibits that bring to life Canada's unique ties with Britain, the US, and France, and explains how the war front affected the home front in Canada. You'll also learn about the heroism of Canadian soldiers and the immense challenges they faced during and after their landings here. You'll see a scrolling list of the 45,000 Canadians who died in WWII, a large hall designed to introduce visitors to the diversity of Canada, and a powerful, 12-minute film about Canada's D-Day experience. During your visit, take advantage of the Centre's eager-to-help, red-shirted "exchange students" (young Canadians who work as guides at the Centre for a 4-month period).

Nearby: Between the main road and the Juno Beach Centre, you'll spot a huge stainless-steel double cross (by a row of French flags). This is La Croix de Lorraine, which marks the site where General de Gaulle landed on June 14, 1944. Information plaques describe this important event, which cemented de Gaulle's role as the leader of free France.

Canadian Cemetery

This small, touching cemetery hides a few miles above the Juno Beach Centre and makes a modest statement when compared with

other, more grandiose cemeteries in this area. To me, it captures the understated nature of Canadians perfectly. Surrounded by beautiful farmland with distant views to the beaches, you'll find 2,000 graves marked with maple leaves and the soldiers' names and age. Some are engraved with family remembrances; all are decorated with live flowers or plants in their honor. You'll also see a few information plaques between the road and the graves.

Getting There: From Courseulles-sur-Mer, follow signs to *Caen* on D-79. After about 2.5 miles (4 kilometers), follow signs to the cemetery (and Bayeux) at the roundabout.

Caen

Though it was mostly destroyed by WWII bombs, today's Caen (pronounced "kahn," population 115,000) is a thriving, workaday city packed with students and a few tourists. The WWII museum and the vibrant old city are the targets for travelers, though these sights come wrapped in a big city with rough edges. And though Bayeux or Arromanches—which are smaller—make the best base for most D-Day sites, train travelers with limited time might find urban Caen more practical because of its buses to Honfleur, convenient car-rental offices near the train station, and easy access to the Caen Memorial Museum.

Orientation to Caen

The looming château, built by William the Conqueror in 1060, marks the city's center. West of here, modern Rue St. Pierre is a popular shopping area and pedestrian zone. To the east, the more historic Vagueux quarter has many restaurants and cafés in half-timbered buildings. A marathon race in honor of the Normandy invasion is held every June 8 and ends at the Memorial Museum.

TOURIST INFORMATION

The TI is opposite the château on Place St. Pierre, 10 long blocks from the train station—take the tram to the St. Pierre stop (Mon-Sat 9:30-18:30, until 19:00 July-Aug, Sun 10:00-13:00 & 14:00-17:00 except closed Sun Oct-March, drivers follow *Parking Château* signs, tel. 02 31 27 14 14, www.tourisme.caen.fr).

ARRIVAL IN CAEN

These directions assume you're headed for the town's main attraction, the Caen Memorial Museum.

By Car: Finding the memorial is quick and easy. It's a half-mile off the ring-road expressway (*périphérique nord*, take *sortie* #7, look for white *Le Mémorial* signs). When leaving the museum, follow *Toutes Directions* signs back to the ring road.

By Train: Caen is two hours from Paris (12/day) and 20 minutes from Bayeux (20/day). Caen's modern train station is next to the *gare routière*, where buses from Honfleur arrive. Car-rental offices are right across the street. There's no baggage storage at the station, though free baggage storage is available at the Caen Memorial Museum. The efficient tramway runs right in front of both stations, and taxis usually wait in front. For detailed instructions on getting to the Caen Memorial Museum, see "Getting There" in the next section.

By Bus: Caen is one hour from Honfleur by express bus (2-3/day), or two hours by the scenic coastal bus (4/day direct). Buses stop near the train station.

Sights in Caen

▲▲Caen Memorial Museum (Le Mémorial de Caen)

Caen, the modern capital of lower Normandy, has the most thorough (and by far the priciest) WWII museum in France. Located

at the site of an important German headquarters during World War II, its official name is The Caen-Normandy Memorial: Center for History and Peace (Le Mémorial de Caen-Normandie: Cité de l'Histoire pour la Paix). With numerous exhibits on the lead-up to World War II, coverage of the war in both Europe and the Pacific, accounts of the Holocaust and Nazi-occupied France, the Cold War aftermath, and more, it effectively puts the Battle of Normandy into a broader context. But it lacks the sharp focus of some of the better D-Day museums at the beaches (such as the Utah Beach Landing Museum). Everything is described well in English.

Cost and Hours: €19, free for all veterans and kids under 10 (ask about good family rates), €20.50 combo-ticket with Arromanches 360° Theater worthwhile if you plan to visit there as well. Open March-Oct daily 9:00-19:00; Nov-Dec and Feb Tue-Sun 9:30-18:00, closed Mon; closed most of Jan; last entry 75 minutes before closing. An €4 audioguide streamlines your visit by providing helpful background for each area of the museum (tel. 02 31 06 06 44—as in June 6, 1944, www.memorial-caen.fr).

Getting There: Taxis normally wait in front of the train station and are the easiest solution (about €15 one-way—more on Sun, 15 minutes), particularly if you have bags.

Allow 30 minutes for the one-way trip via **tram and bus.** Take the tram right in front of the station (line A, direction: Campus 2, or line B, direction: St. Clair; buy €1.30 ticket from machine, good for entire trip, validate it on tram—white side up—and again on bus when you transfer). Get off at the third tram stop (Bernières), then transfer to frequent bus #2 (signed from the tram stop). For transit maps, see www.twisto.fr.

Returning from the museum by bus and tram is a snap (taxi there and bus/tram back is a good compromise). Bus #2 stops across from the museum on the street's right side (the museum has the schedule, buy ticket from driver and validate). The bus whisks you to the Quatrans stop in downtown Caen where you'll transfer to the tram next to the bus stop. Either line A or line B will take you to the station—get off at the Gare SNCF stop.

Services: The museum provides free baggage storage and free supervised babysitting for children under 10 (for whom exhibits may be too graphic). There's a large gift shop with plenty of books in English, a reasonable all-day sandwich shop/café above the entry area, and a restaurant with a garden-side terrace (lunch only). Picnicking in the gardens is also an option.

Minivan Tours: The museum offers good-value minivan tours covering the key sites along the D-Day beaches. Two identical half-day tours leave the museum: one at 9:00 (€65/person) and one at 13:00 or 14:00—depending on the season (€82/person); both include entry to the museum. The all-day "D-Day Tour" package (€117) is designed for day-trippers and includes pick-up from the Caen train station (with frequent service from Paris), a tour of the Caen Memorial Museum followed by lunch, then a five-hour tour in English of the American sector. Your day ends with a drop-off at the Caen train station in time to catch a train back to Paris or elsewhere. Canadians have a similar €117 tour option to Juno Beach. Contact the museum for details and reservations.

Planning Your Museum Time: Allow two hours for your visit. The museum is divided into two major wings: the "World Before 1945" (the lead-up to World War II and the battles and related events of the war), and the "World After 1945" (Cold War). I'd focus on the "World Before 1945." Pick up the map as you enter, and be sure to check out any special exhibitions. Pace yourself—there's a lot to see.

Visiting the Museum: Begin by watching *Jour J (D-Day)*, an old-fashioned 15-minute film that shows the build-up to D-Day (runs every 30 minutes from 10:00 to 18:00, works in any language). Although snippets come from the movie *The Longest Day* and German army training films, some footage is of actual battle scenes.

On the opposite side of the entry hall from the theater, find *Début de la Visite* signs and begin your museum tour with a downward-spiral stroll, tracing (almost psychoanalyzing) the path Europe followed from the end of World War I to the rise of fascism to World War II.

The **"World Before 1945"** exhibit, on the lower level, gives a thorough look at how World War II was fought—from General Charles de Gaulle's London radio broadcasts to Hitler's early missiles to wartime fashion to the D-Day landings. Videos, maps, and countless displays relate the war's many side stories, including the

Battle of Britain, the French Resistance, Vichy France, German death camps, the Battle of Stalingrad, and the war in the Pacific. Several powerful exhibits summarize the terrible human costs of World War II (Russia alone saw 21 million of its people die during the war; the US lost 300,000). A smaller, separate exhibit (on your way back up to the main hall) covers just D-Day and the Battle of Normandy.

The **"World After 1945"** wing sets the scene for the Cold War with photos of European cities destroyed during World War II. It continues with a helpful overview of the bipolar world that followed the war, with insights into the psychological battle waged by the Soviet Union and the US for the hearts and minds of their people until the fall of communism. The wing culminates with a major display recounting the division of Berlin and its unification after the fall of the Wall.

Two more worthwhile stops are outside (exit below the cafeteria, then climb down the stairs). First, you can walk through the former **command bunker** of German General Wilhelm Richter, where you'll see exhibits on the Nazi "Atlantic Wall" defense in Normandy—for which Richter was in charge.

The finale is a walk through the **US Armed Forces Memorial Garden** (Vallée du Mémorial). On a visit here, I was bothered at first by the seemingly mindless laughing of lighthearted children, unable to appreciate the gravity of their surroundings. Then I read this inscription on the pavement: "From the heart of our land flows the blood of our youth, given to you in the name of freedom." And their laughter made me happy.

Mont St-Michel

For more than a thousand years, the distant silhouette of this island abbey sent pilgrims' spirits soaring. Today, it does the same for tourists. Mont St-Michel, among the top four pilgrimage sites in Christendom through the ages, floats like a mirage on the horizon. Today, several million visitors—far more tourists than pilgrims— flood the single street of the tiny island each year.

In 2015, Mont St-Michel wrapped up a multiyear engineering project to replace the old causeway with a modern bridge, improving water circulation in the bay (see sidebar). With the work finally done, now is a great time to visit.

Orientation to Mont St-Michel

Mont St-Michel is surrounded by a vast mudflat and connected to the mainland by a bridge. Think of the island as having three parts: the fortified abbey soaring above, the petite village squatting in the middle, and the lower-level medieval fortifications. The village has just one main street, on which you'll find all the hotels, restaurants, and trinkets. Between 11:00 and 16:00, tourists trample the dreamscape (much like pilgrims did 800 years ago). A ramble on the ramparts offers mudflat views and an escape from the tourist zone. Though several tacky history-in-wax museums tempt visitors, the only worthwhile sights are the abbey at the summit of the island and views from the ramparts and quieter lanes as you descend.

Daytime Mont St-Michel is a touristy gauntlet—worth a stop, but a short one will do. To avoid crowds, arrive late, sleep on the island or nearby on the mainland, and depart early. To bypass the tacky souvenir shops and human traffic jam on the main drag, follow the detour path up or down the mount. The tourist tide recedes late each afternoon. On nights from autumn through spring, the island stands serene, its floodlit abbey towering above a sleepy village. The abbey interior is open until midnight from mid-July to the end of August (Mon-Sat only).

The "village" on the mainland side of the causeway (called La Caserne) consists of a lineup of modern hotels and a handful of shops.

TOURIST INFORMATION

On the mainland, near the parking lot's shuttle stop, look for the excellent wood-and-glass **visitors center,** which has slick touchscreen monitors describing the various phases of the causeway project, free WCs and luggage lockers, and information about Normandy and Brittany (daily April-Sept 9:00-19:00, off-season 10:00-18:00). The visitors center can be less crowded than the island's helpful official **TI,** which is on your left as you enter Mont St-Michel's gates (daily July-Aug 9:00-19:00, March-June and Sept-Oct 9:00-12:30 & 14:00-18:00, Nov-Feb 10:00-12:30 & 14:00-17:00; tel. 02 33 60 14 30, www.ot-montsaintmichel.com). A post office and ATM are 50 yards beyond the TI.

Either office is a good place to ask about English tour times for the abbey, bus schedules, and the tide table *(Horaires des Marées),* which is essential if you plan to explore the mudflats.

An Island Again

In 1878, a causeway was built that allowed Mont St-Michel's pilgrims to come and go regardless of the tide (and without hip boots). The causeway increased the flow of visitors, but blocked the flow of water around the island. The result: Much of the bay silted up, and Mont St-Michel was no longer an island.

An ambitious project to return the island to its original form was completed in 2015. The first phase, in 2010, saw the construction of a dam (*barrage*) on the Couesnon River, which traps water at high tide and releases it at low tide, flushing the bay and forcing sediment out to the sea. The dam is an attraction in its own right, with informative panels and great views of the abbey from its sleek wood benches). Parking lots at the foot of the island were removed and a huge mainland parking lot was built, with shuttle buses to take visitors to the island.

In 2014, workers tore down the old causeway and replaced it with the super-sleek bridge you see today. This allowed water to flow underneath the bridge, and Mont St-Michel became an island once again.

ARRIVAL IN MONT ST-MICHEL

Prepare for lots of walking, particularly if you arrive by car and are not sleeping on the island or in nearby La Caserne.

By Train: The nearest train station is five miles away in Pontorson (called Pontorson-Mont St-Michel). The few trains that stop here are met by a bus waiting to take passengers right to the gates of Mont St-Michel (€3.20, 12 buses/day July-Aug, 8/day Sept-June, fewer on Sun, 20 minutes, tel. 02 14 13 20 15, www.accueilmontsaintmichel.com). Taxis between Pontorson and Mont St-Michel get you to the *navette* (island shuttle) stop and cost about €20 (€25 after 19:00 and on weekends/holidays; tel. 02 33 60 33 23 or 02 33 60 82 70). If you plan to arrive on Saturday night, beware that Sunday train service from Pontorson is almost nonexistent.

By Bus: Buses from Rennes and St-Malo stop next to the TI at the parking lot. From Bayeux, it's faster by shuttle van.

By Car: If you're staying at a hotel on the island, follow signs for *La Caserne* and enter the parking lot on your right. Parking P3 is for you (€12.50). Those staying in La Caserne can drive right to their hotel, but you need a code number to open a gate blocking the access road (generally €4/entry; get code and directions from your hotelier before you arrive).

Day-trippers are directed to a sea of parking (see map)—like arriving at an amusement park, you'll have to follow signs to the section that's currently open. To avoid extra walking, take your parking ticket with you and pay at the machines near the TI when

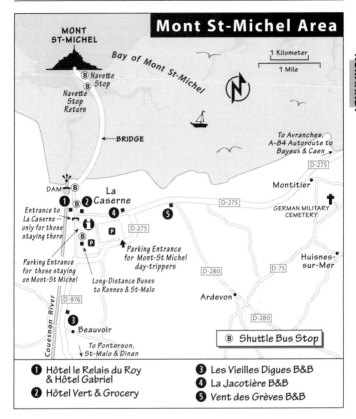

Mont St-Michel Area

MONT ST-MICHEL

Bay of Mont St-Michel

1 Kilometer

1 Mile

B Navette Stop
B Navette Stop
Navette Stop Return

BRIDGE

To Avranches, A-84 Autoroute to Bayeux & Caen

D-275

Montitier

DAM B
La Caserne
Entrance to La Caserne -- only for those staying there
Parking Entrance for those staying on Mont-St Michel

D-275

GERMAN MILITARY CEMETERY

Parking Entrance for Mont-St Michel day-trippers

Long-Distance Buses to Rennes & St-Malo

Huisnes-sur-Mer

D-280   D-75

Ardevon

D-280

Couesnon River

D-976

Beauvoir

To Pontorson, St-Malo & Dinan

B Shuttle Bus Stop

❶ Hôtel le Relais du Roy & Hôtel Gabriel
❷ Hôtel Vert & Grocery
❸ Les Vieilles Digues B&B
❹ La Jacotière B&B
❺ Vent des Grèves B&B

you leave (€12.50 flat fee, good for 24 hours but no re-entry privileges, machines accept cash and US credit cards, parking tel. 02 14 13 20 15). If you arrive after 19:00 and stay only for the evening, parking is free. If you arrive after 19:00 and leave before 11:30 in the morning, the fee is €4.30.

From the remote parking lot or *La Caserne* village, you can either walk to the island or take the short ride on the free shuttle (departures every few minutes). The shuttle stops at the parking lot visitors center, near the hotels in the village, near the dam at the start of the bridge, and at the island itself, with ideal views of Mont St-Michel. The return shuttle picks up about a hundred yards farther from the island (look for benches along the road). You can also ride either way in the horse-drawn *maringote* (double-decker wagon, €5.30).

HELPFUL HINTS

Tides: The tides here rise above 50 feet—the largest and most dangerous in Europe. High tides *(grandes marées)* lap against the TI door, where you should find tide hours posted.

Groceries: Next to **Hôtel Vert** in La Caserne is a misnamed Super Marché stocked with souvenirs and some groceries (daily 9:00-20:00).

Taxi: Call 02 33 60 33 23 or 02 33 60 26 89.

Guided Tours: Several top-notch guides can lead you through the abbey's complex history. The best are found in Bayeux, a good base for a day trip to Mont St-Michel. **Westcapades** provides transportation from St-Malo or Rennes with background commentary (tel. 02 23 23 01 96, www.westcapades. com, marc@westcapades.com).

Guided Walks: The TI can refer you to companies that run inexpensive guided walks across the bay (with some English).

Crowd-Beating Tips: If you're staying overnight, arrive after 16:00 and leave by 11:00 to avoid the worst crowds. The island's main drag is wall-to-wall people from 11:00 to 16:00. Bypass this mess by following this book's suggested walking routes (under "Sights in Mont St-Michel"); the *gendarmerie* shortcut works best if you want to avoid both crowds and stairs.

Best Light: Because Mont St-Michel faces southwest, morning light from the bridge is eye-popping. Take a memorable walk before breakfast. And don't miss the illuminated island after dark (also best from the bridge).

Sights in Mont St-Michel

These sights are listed in the order by which you approach them from the mainland.

The Bay of Mont St-Michel

The vast Bay of Mont St-Michel has long played a key role. Since the sixth century, hermit-monks in search of solitude lived here. The word "hermit" comes from an ancient Greek word meaning "desert." The next best thing to a desert in this part of Europe was the sea. Imagine the desert this bay provided as the first monk climbed the rock to get close to God. Add to that the mythic tide, which sends the surf speeding eight miles in and out with each lunar cycle. Long before the original causeway was built, when Mont St-Michel was an island, pilgrims would approach across the mudflat, aware that the tide swept in "at the speed of a galloping horse" (well, maybe a trotting horse—12 mph, or about 18 feet per second at top speed).

Quicksand was another peril. A short stroll onto the sticky

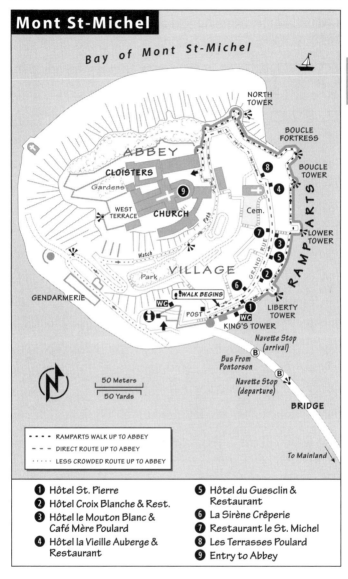

Mont St-Michel

Bay of Mont St-Michel

NORTH TOWER

BOUCLE FORTRESS

BOUCLE TOWER

ABBEY

CLOISTERS

Gardens

WEST TERRACE

CHURCH

Cem.

LOWER TOWER

RAMPARTS

Watch

VILLAGE

Park

GENDARMERIE

WALK BEGINS

WC

POST

WC

LIBERTY TOWER

KING'S TOWER

Navette Stop (arrival)

Bus From Pontorson

B

Navette Stop (departure)

B

BRIDGE

50 Meters

50 Yards

To Mainland

- - - RAMPARTS WALK UP TO ABBEY
- - DIRECT ROUTE UP TO ABBEY
····· LESS CROWDED ROUTE UP TO ABBEY

❶ Hôtel St. Pierre
❷ Hôtel Croix Blanche & Rest.
❸ Hôtel le Mouton Blanc & Café Mère Poulard
❹ Hôtel la Vieille Auberge & Restaurant

❺ Hôtel du Guesclin & Restaurant
❻ La Sirène Crêperie
❼ Restaurant le St. Michel
❽ Les Terrasses Poulard
❾ Entry to Abbey

sand helps you imagine how easy it would be to get one or both feet stuck as the tide rolled in. The greater danger for adventurers today is the thoroughly disorienting fog and the fact that the sea can encircle unwary hikers. (Bring a mobile phone, and if you're stuck, dial 112.) Braving these devilish risks for centuries, pilgrims kept their eyes on the spire crowned by their protector, St. Michael, and eventually reached their spiritual goal.

▲▲Mudflat Stroll Around Mont St-Michel

To resurrect that Mont St-Michel dreamscape, it's possible to walk out on the mudflats that surround the island. At low tide, it's reasonably dry and a great memory-maker. But it can be hazardous, so don't go alone, don't stray far, and be sure to double-check the tides—or consider a guided walk (details at the TI). Remember the scene from the Bayeux tapestry where Harold rescues the Normans from the quicksand? It happened somewhere in this bay.

The Village Below the Abbey

The island's main street (Rue Principale, or "Grande Rue"), lined with shops and hotels leading to the abbey, is grotesquely touristy.

It is some consolation to remember that, even in the Middle Ages, this was a commercial gauntlet, with stalls selling souvenir medallions, candles, and fast food. With only 30 full-time residents, the village lives solely for tourists. If crowds stick in your craw, keep left as you enter the island, passing under the stone arch of the *gendarmerie,* and follow the cobbled ramp up to the abbey. This is also the easiest route up, thanks to the long ramps, which help you avoid most stairs. (Others should follow the directions below, which still avoid most crowds.)

After visiting the TI, check the tide warnings (posted on the wall) and pass through the imposing doors. Before the drawbridge, on your left, peek through the door of Restaurant la Mère Poulard. The original Madame Poulard (the maid of an abbey architect who married the village baker) made quick and tasty omelets here *(omelette tradition).* These were popular for pilgrims who, before the causeway (or bridge) was built, needed to beat the tide to get out. They're still a hit with tourists—even at the rip-off price they charge today (they're much cheaper elsewhere). Pop in for a minute just to enjoy the show as old-time-costumed cooks beat eggs.

You could continue the grueling trudge uphill to the abbey with the masses (all island hotel receptions are located on this street). But if the abbey's your goal, bypass the worst crowds and tourist kitsch by climbing the first steps on your right after the drawbridge and follow the ramparts in either direction up and up to the abbey (quieter if you go right).

Public WCs are next to the island TI at the town entry, after the Mère Poulard Biscuiterie on the right, and partway up the main drag by the tiny St. Pierre church, where you can attend Mass (times posted on the door), opposite Les Terrasses Poulard gift shop.

▲▲Abbey of Mont St-Michel

Mont St-Michel has been an important pilgrimage center since A.D. 708, when the bishop of Avranches heard the voice of Archangel Michael saying, "Build here and build high." With the foresight of a saint, Michael reassured the bishop, "If you build it...they will come." Today's abbey is built on the remains of a Romanesque church, which stands on the remains of a Carolingian church. St. Michael, whose gilded statue decorates the top of the spire, was the patron saint of many French kings, making this a favored site for French royalty through the ages. St. Michael was particularly popular in Counter-Reformation times, as the Church employed his warlike image in the fight against Protestant heresy.

This abbey has 1,200 years of history, though much of its story was lost when its archives were taken to St-Lô for safety during World War II—only to be destroyed during the D-Day fighting. As you climb the stairs, imagine the centuries of pilgrims and monks who have worn down the edges of these same stone steps. Keep to the right, as tour groups can clog the left side of the steps.

Cost and Hours: €9; May-mid-July daily 9:00-19:00; mid-July-Aug Mon-Sat 9:00-24:00, Sun 9:00-19:00; Sept-April daily 9:30-18:00; closed Dec 25, Jan 1, and May 1; last entry one hour before closing, mid-July-Aug ticket office closes from 18:00-18:30; www.mont-saint-michel.monuments-nationaux.fr/en. Buy your ticket to the abbey and keep climbing. Mass is held Mon-Sat at 12:00, Sun at 11:15, in the abbey church (www.abbaye-montsaintmichel.com).

Visiting the Abbey: Allow 15 minutes to hike at a steady pace from the island TI. To avoid crowds, arrive by 10:00 or after 16:00 (the place gets really busy by 11:00). On most summer evenings, when the abbey is open until 24:00 and crowds are gone, visits come with music and mood lighting called *Ballades Nocturnes* (€9, none held Sun). It's worth paying a second admission to see the abbey so peaceful (nighttime program starts at 19:00; daytime tickets aren't valid for re-entry, but you can visit before 19:00 and stay on).

Tours: Get an English leaflet and follow my self-guided tour below. The excellent audioguide gives greater detail (€4.50, €6/2 people). You can also take a 1.25-hour English-language guided tour (free but tip requested, 2-4 tours/day, first and last tours usually around 11:00—or 10:45 on Sun—and 15:00, confirm times at TI, meet at top terrace in front of church). The guided tours, which can be good, come with big crowds. You can start a tour, then decide if it works for you—but I'd skip it, instead following my directions, next.

Ↄ Self-Guided Tour: Visit the abbey by following a one-way route. You'll climb to the ticket office, then climb some more. Stop after you pass a public WC, and look back to the church. That boxy Gothic structure across the steps is one of six cisterns that provided the abbey with water. Go through the room marked *Accueil,* with interesting models of the abbey through the ages.

• *Emerging on the other side, find your way to the big terrace, walk to the round lookout at the far end, and face the church.*

West Terrace: In 1776, a fire destroyed the west end of the church, leaving this grand view terrace. The original extent of the church is outlined with short walls. In the paving stones, notice the stonecutter numbers, which are generally not exposed like this—a reminder that they were paid by the piece. The buildings of Mont St-Michel are made of granite stones quarried from the Isles of Chausey (visible on a clear day, 20 miles away). Tidal power was ingeniously harnessed to load, unload, and even transport the stones, as barges hitched a ride with each incoming tide.

As you survey the Bay of Mont St-Michel, notice the polder land—farmland reclaimed by Normans in the 19th century with the help of Dutch engineers. The lines of trees mark strips of land used in the process. Today, this reclaimed land is covered by salt-loving plants and grazed by sheep whose salty meat is considered a local treat. You're standing 240 feet above sea level, at the summit of what was an island called "the big tomb." The small island just farther out is "the little tomb."

The bay stretches from Normandy (on the right as you look to the sea) to Brittany (on the left). The Couesnon River below marks the historic border between the two lands. Brittany and Normandy have long vied for Mont St-Michel. In fact, the river used to pass Mont St-Michel on the other side, making the abbey part of Brittany. Today, it's just barely—but definitively—on Norman soil. The new dam across this river (easy to see from here—it looks like a bridge when its gates are open) was built in 2010. Central to the dam is a system of locking gates that retain water upriver during high tide and release it six hours later, in effect flushing the bay and returning it to a mudflat at low tide.

• *Now enter the...*

Abbey Church: Sit on a pew near the altar, under the little statue of the Archangel Michael (with the spear to defeat dragons and evil, and the scales to evaluate your soul). Monks built the church on the tip of this rock to be as close to heaven as possible. The downside: There wasn't enough level ground to support a sizable abbey and church. The solution: Four immense crypts were built under the church to create a platform to support each of its wings. While most of the church is Romanesque (round arches, 11th century), the light-filled apse behind the altar was built later, when Gothic arches were the rage. In 1421, the crypt that supported the apse collapsed, taking that end of the church with it. Few of the original windows survive (victims of fires, storms, lightning, and the Revolution).

In the chapel to the right of the altar stands a grim-looking statue of the man with the vision to build the abbey (St. Aubert). Take a spin around the apse and find the suspended pirate-looking ship. Directly in front of the altar, look for the glass-covered manhole (you'll see it again later from another angle).

• *Continue looping around the church, then follow* Suite de la Visite *signs to enter the...*

Cloisters: A standard feature of an abbey, this was the peaceful zone that connected various rooms, where monks could meditate, read the Bible, and tend their gardens (growing food and herbs for medicine). The great view window is enjoyable today (what's the tide doing?), but it was of no use to the monks. The more secluded a monk could be, the closer he was to God. (A cloister, by definition, is an enclosed place.) Notice how the columns are staggered. This efficient design allowed the cloisters to be supported with less building material (a top priority, given the difficulty of transporting stone this high up). The carvings above the columns feature various plants and heighten the Garden-of-Eden ambience the cloister offered the monks. The statues of various saints, carved among some columns, were de-faced—literally—by French revolutionaries.

• *Continue on to the...*

Refectory: This was the dining hall where the monks consumed both food and the word of God in silence—one monk read in a monotone from the Bible during meals (pulpit on the right near the far end). The monks gathered as a family here in one undivided space under one big arch (an impressive engineering feat in its day). The abbot ate at the head table; guests sat at the table in the middle. The clever columns are thin but very deep, allowing maximum light while offering solid support. From 966 until 2001, this was a Benedictine abbey. In 2001, the last three Benedictine monks checked out, and a new order of monks from Paris took over.

• *Stairs lead down one flight to a...*

Round Stone Relief of St. Michael: This scene depicts the legend of Mont St-Michel: The archangel Michael wanted to commemorate a hard-fought victory over the devil with the construction of a monumental abbey on a nearby island. He chose to send his message to the bishop of Avranches (St. Aubert), who saw Michael twice in his dreams. But the bishop did not trust his dreams until the third time, when Michael drove his thumb into the bishop's head, leaving a mark that he could not deny.

• *Continue down the stairs another flight to the...*

Guests' Hall: St. Benedict wrote that guests should be welcomed according to their status. That meant that when kings (or other VIPs) visited, they were wined and dined without a hint of monastic austerity. This room once exploded in color, with gold stars on a blue sky across the ceiling. (This room's decoration was said to be the model for Sainte-Chapelle in Paris.) The floor was composed of glazed red-and-green tiles. The entire space was bathed in glorious sunlight, made divine as it passed through a filter of stained glass. The big double fireplace, kept out of sight by hanging tapestries, served as a kitchen—walk under it and see the light.

• *Hike up the stairs through a chapel to the...*

Hall of the Grand Pillars: Perched on a pointy rock, the huge abbey church had four sturdy crypts like this to prop it up. You're standing under the Gothic portion of the abbey church—this was the crypt that collapsed in 1421. Notice the immensity of the columns (15 feet around) in the new crypt, rebuilt with a determination not to let it fall again. Now look up at the round hole in the ceiling and recognize it as the glass "manhole cover" from the church altar above.

• *To see what kind of crypt collapsed, continue on to the...*

Crypt of St. Martin: This simple 11th-century Romanesque vault has minimal openings, since the walls needed to be solid and fat to support the buildings above. As you leave, notice the thickness of the walls.

• *Next, you'll find the...*

Ossuary (identifiable by its big treadwheel): The monks celebrated death as well as life. This part of the abbey housed the hospital, morgue, and ossuary. Because the abbey graveyard was small, it was routinely emptied, and the bones were stacked here.

During the Revolution, monasticism was abolished. Church property was taken by the atheistic government, and from 1793 to 1863, Mont St-Michel was used as an Alcatraz-type prison. Its first inmates were 300 priests who refused to renounce their vows. (Victor Hugo complained that using such a place as a prison was like keeping a toad in a reliquary.) The big treadwheel—the kind that did heavy lifting for big building projects throughout the Middle Ages—is from the decades when the abbey was a prison. Teams of six prisoners marched two abreast in the wheel—hamster-style—powering two-ton loads of stone and supplies up Mont St-Michel. Spin the rollers of the sled next to the wheel.

From here, you'll pass through a chapel, walk up the Romanesque-arched North-South Stairs, walk through the Promenade of the Monks, go under more Gothic vaults, and finally descend into the vast **Scriptorium Hall** (a.k.a. Knights Hall), where monks decorated illuminated manuscripts. You'll then spiral down to the gift shop, exiting out the back door (follow signs to the *Jardins*).

• *You'll emerge into the rear garden. From here, look up at a miracle of medieval engineering.*

The "Merveille": This was an immense building project—a marvel back in 1220. Three levels of buildings were created: the lower floor for the lower class, the middle floor for VIPs, and the top floor for the clergy. It was a medieval skyscraper, built with the social strata in mind. The vision was even grander—the place where you're standing was to be built up in similar fashion, to support a further expansion of the church. But the money ran out, and the project was abandoned. As you leave the garden, notice the tall narrow windows of the refectory on the top floor.

• *Stairs lead from here back into the village. To avoid the crowds on your descent, turn right when you see the knee-high sign for* Musée Historique *and find your own route down or, at the same place, follow the* Chemin des Ramparts *to the left and hike down via the...*

Ramparts: Mont St-Michel is ringed by a fine example of 15th-century fortifications. They were built to defend against a new weapon: the cannon. They were low, rather than tall—to make a smaller target—and connected by protected passageways, which enabled soldiers to zip quickly to whichever zone was under attack. The five-sided Boucle Tower (1481) was crafted with no blind angles, so defenders could protect it and the nearby walls in all directions. And though the English conquered all of Normandy in the early 15th century, they never took this well-fortified island. Because of its stubborn success against the English in the Hundred Years' War, Mont St-Michel became a symbol of French national identity.

After dark, the island is magically floodlit. Views from the ramparts are sublime. But for the best view, exit the island and walk out on the bridge a few hundred yards.

NEAR MONT ST-MICHEL
German Military Cemetery (Cimetière Militaire Allemand)
Located three miles from Mont St-Michel, near tiny Huisnes-sur-Mer (well-signed east of Mont St-Michel, off D-275), this somber but thoughtfully presented cemetery-mortuary houses the remains of 12,000 German WWII soldiers brought to this location from all over France. (The stone blocks on the steps up indicate the regions in France from where they came.) A display of letters they sent home (with English translations) offers insights into the soldiers' lives. From the lookout, take in the sensational views over Mont St-Michel.

Sleeping in Mont St-Michel

Sleep on or near the island so that you can visit Mont St-Michel early and late. What matters is being here before or after the crush of tourists. Sleeping on the island—inside the walls—is a great experience for medieval romantics who don't mind the headaches associated with spending a night here, including average rooms and baggage hassles. To reach a room on the island, you'll need to carry your bags 10 minutes uphill from the *navette* (shuttle) stop. Take only what you need for one night in a smaller bag, but don't leave any luggage visible in your car.

Hotels near the island in *La Caserne* are a good deal cheaper and require less walking—you can park right at your hotel. All are a short walk from the free and frequent shuttle to the island, allowing easy access at any time.

ON THE ISLAND

There are eight small hotels on the island, and because most visitors day-trip here, finding a room is generally no problem (but finding an elevator is). Though some pad their profits by requesting that guests buy dinner from their restaurant, *requiring* it is illegal. Higher-priced rooms generally have bay views. Several hotels are closed from November until Easter.

The following hotels are listed in order of altitude; the first hotels are lowest.

$$$ Hôtel St. Pierre* and **Hôtel Croix Blanche***,** which share the same owners and reception desk, sit side by side (reception at St. Pierre). Each provides comfortable rooms at inflated prices, some with good views. Both have several family loft rooms (nonview Db-€220, view Db-€225, Tb or Qb-€270-300; lower rates for Hôtel Croix Blanche; breakfast-€17, tel. 02 33 60 14 03, www.auberge-saint-pierre.fr, contact@auberge-saint-pierre.fr).

$$$ Hôtel le Mouton Blanc** delivers a fair midrange value, with 15 rooms split between two buildings. The main building *(bâtiment principal)* is best, with cozy rooms, wood beams, and decent bathrooms; the more modern "annex" has cramped bathrooms (Db-€145, loft Tb-€160, loft Qb-€195, breakfast-€17, tel. 02 33 60 14 08, www.lemoutonblanc.fr, contact@lemoutonblanc.fr).

$$$ Hôtel la Vieille Auberge** is a small place with sharp rooms at fair prices (Db-€130, Tb-€180; spring for one of the four great terrace rooms—Db-€165; breakfast-€17, check in at their restaurant, but book through Hôtel St. Pierre, listed above).

$$ Hôtel du Guesclin** has the cheapest and best-value rooms I list on the island and is the only family-run hotel left there. Rooms have traditional decor and are perfectly comfortable. Check in at reception one floor up; if no one's there, try the bar on the main-street level (Db-€90-105, Tb-105-130, breakfast-€10, tel. 02 33 60 14 10, www.hotelduguesclin.com, hotel.duguesclin@ wanadoo.fr).

ON THE MAINLAND

Modern hotels gather in La Caserne on the mainland. These have soulless but cheaper rooms with easy parking (€4 access fee for entering La Caserne) and many tour groups. Remember to call at least a day ahead to get the code allowing you to skip the parking lot and drive to your hotel's front door.

$$$ Hôtel le Relais du Roy*** houses small but well-configured and plush rooms. Most rooms are on the riverside, with nice countryside views, and many have small balconies allowing "lean-out" views to the abbey (Db-€90-125, bar, restaurant, breakfast-€11, tel. 02 33 60 14 25, www.le-relais-du-roy.com, reservation@le-relais-du-roy.com).

$$$ Hôtel Gabriel*** has 45 modern rooms, both bright and tight, with flashy colors and fair rates (Db-€110-131, extra person-€21, includes breakfast, tel. 02 33 60 14 13, www.hotelgabriel-montsaintmichel.com, hotelgabriel@le-mont-saint-michel.com).

$$ Hôtel Vert** provides 54 motel-esque rooms at good rates (Db-€69-89, extra person-€20, breakfast-€9, tel. 02 33 60 09 33, www.hotelvert-montsaintmichel.com, stmichel@le-mont-saint-michel.com).

CHAMBRES D'HOTES

Simply great values, these converted farmhouses are a few minutes' drive from the island.

$$ Les Vieilles Digues, where charming, English-speaking Danielle and Kin will pamper you, is two miles toward Pontorson on the main road (on the left if you're coming from Mont St-Michel). It has a lovely garden and seven homey, borderline-kitschy rooms with subtle Asian touches, all with showers (but no Mont St-Michel views). Ground-floor rooms have patios on the garden (D with private bathroom across hall-€80, Db-€85, Tb-€105, includes good breakfast, easy parking—and you can walk to the free shuttle at the main parking lot, 68 Route du Mont St-Michel, tel. 02 33 58 55 30, www.bnb-normandy.com, danielle.tchen@ wanadoo.fr).

$$ La Jacotière is closest to Mont St-Michel and within walking distance of the regional bus stop and the shuttle (allowing you to avoid the €12.50 fee to park). Gérald and Alicia, a charming young couple, offer six immaculate rooms and views of the island from the backyard (Db-€85, studio with great view from private patio-€90, extra bed-€20, big family room for up to 4 people-€125, includes breakfast, tel. 02 33 60 22 94, www.lajacotiere.

fr, la.jacotiere@wanadoo.fr). Drivers coming from Bayeux should turn off the road just prior to the main parking lot. As the road bends to the left away from the bay, look for a regional-products store standing alone on the right. Take the small lane in front of the store signed *sauf véhicule autorisé*—La Jacotière is the next building.

$ Vent des Grèves is about a mile down D-275 from Mont St-Michel (green sign; if arriving from the north, it's just after Auberge de la Baie). Sweet Estelle (who speaks English) offers five bright, big, and modern rooms with good views of Mont St-Michel and a common deck with tables to let you soak it all in (Sb-€42, Db-€52, Tb-€62, Qb-€72, includes breakfast, tel. 02 33 48 28 89, www.ventdesgreves.com, ventdesgreves@orange.fr).

Eating in Mont St-Michel

Puffy omelets (*omelette montoise,* or *omelette tradition*) are Mont St-Michel's specialty. Also look for mussels (best with crème fraîche), seafood platters, and locally raised lamb *pré-salé* (a saltwater-grass diet gives the meat a unique taste, but beware of impostor lamb from New Zealand—ask where your dinner was raised). Muscadet wine (dry, white, and cheap) from the western Loire valley is made nearby and goes well with most regional dishes.

The menus at most of the island's restaurants look like carbon copies of one another (with *menus* from €18 to €28, cheap crêpes, and full à la carte choices). Some places have better views or more appealing decor, and a few have outdoor seating with views along the ramparts walk—ideal when it's sunny. If it's too cool to sit outside, window-shop the places that face the bay from the ramparts walk and arrive early to land a bay-view table. Unless noted otherwise, the listed restaurants are open daily for lunch and dinner.

La Sirène Crêperie offers a good island value and a cozy interior (€9 main-course crêpes, open daily for lunch, open for dinner in summer only, closed Fri off-season, enter through gift shop across from Hôtel St. Pierre, tel. 02 33 60 08 60).

Hôtel du Guesclin is the top place for a traditional meal, with white tablecloths and beautiful views of the bay from its inside-only tables (closed Thu, book a window table in advance; see details under "Sleeping in Mont St-Michel—On the Island," earlier).

Restaurant le St. Michel is lighthearted, reasonable, family-friendly, and run by helpful Patricia (decent omelets, mussels, salads, and pasta; open daily for lunch only, closed Thu-Fri off-season, open for dinner in July-Aug, test its toilet in the rock, across from Hôtel le Mouton Blanc, tel. 02 33 60 14 37).

Café Mère Poulard is a stylish three-story café-*crêperie*-restaurant one door up from Hôtel le Mouton Blanc. It's worth considering for its upstairs terrace, which offers the best outside table views up to the abbey (when their umbrellas don't block it). **La Vieille Auberge** has a broad terrace with the next-best views to the abbey and, so far, no big umbrellas. **La Croix Blanche** owns a small deck with abbey views and window-front tables with bay views, and **Les Terrasses Poulard** has indoor views to the bay.

Picnics: This is the romantic's choice. The small lanes above the main street hide scenic picnic spots, such as the small park at the base of the ancient treadwheel ramp to the upper abbey. You'll catch late sun by following the ramp that leads you through the *gendarmerie* and down behind the island (on the left as you face the main entry to the island). Sandwiches, pizza by the slice, salads, and drinks are all available to go at shops along the main drag. But you'll find a better selection at the modest Super Marché located on the mainland.

Mont St-Michel Connections

BY TRAIN, BUS, OR TAXI

Bus and train service to Mont St-Michel is a challenge. Depending on where you're coming from, you may find that you're forced to arrive and depart early or late—leaving you with too much or too little time on the island.

From Mont St-Michel to Paris: There are several ways to get to Paris. Most travelers take the regional bus from Mont St-Michel to Rennes or Dol-de-Bretagne and connect directly to the TGV (4/day via Rennes, 1/day via Dol-de-Bretagne, 4 hours total via either route from Mont St-Michel to Paris' Gare Montparnasse; €15 for bus to Rennes, €8 for bus to Dol-de-Bretagne; not covered by rail pass, buy ticket from driver, all explained in English at www.destination-montstmichel.com). You can also take a short bus ride to Pontorson (see next) and catch one of a very few trains from there (3/day, 5.5 hours, transfer in Caen, St-Malo, or Rennes).

From Mont St-Michel to Pontorson: The nearest train station to Mont St-Michel is five miles away, in Pontorson (called Pontorson/Mont St-Michel). It's connected to Mont St-Michel by bus or by taxi (see details earlier, under "Arrival in Mont St-Michel").

From Pontorson by Train to: Bayeux (2-3/day, 2 hours; faster by shuttle van).

From Mont St-Michel by Bus to: St-Malo (1/day direct, 1.5 hours, daily July-Aug, less off-season, €22 round-trip fare even if only going one-way, buy from driver; or take 16:10 bus to Dol-de-Bretagne then train to St-Malo, 1.5 hours), **Rennes** (4/day direct, 2 hours). Keolis buses provide service to St-Malo, Dol-de-Bretagne, and Rennes (tel. 02 99 19 70 70, www.keolis-emeraude.com/en).

Taxis are more expensive, but are helpful when trains and buses don't cooperate. Figure €90 from Mont St-Michel to St-Malo, and €100 to Dinan (50 percent more on Sun and at night).

BY CAR

From Mont St-Michel to St-Malo, Brittany: The direct (and free) freeway route takes 40 minutes. For a scenic drive into Brittany, take the following route: Head to Pontorson, follow *D-19* signs to St-Malo, then look for *St. Malo par la Côte* and join D-797, which leads along *La Route de la Baie* to D-155 and on to the oyster capital of Cancale. In Cancale, keep tracking *St. Malo par la Côte* and *Route de la Baie* signs. You'll be routed through the town's port (good lunch stop),

then emerge on D-201. Take time to savor Pointe du Grouin, then continue west on D-201 as it hugs the coast to St-Malo.

From Mont St-Michel to Bayeux: Take the free and zippy A-84 toward Caen, exit at St. Lô, then follow signs to Bayeux.

PRACTICALITIES

This section covers just the basics on traveling in France (for much more information, see the latest edition of *Rick Steves France*). You'll find free advice on specific topics at www.ricksteves.com/tips.

The Language

In France, it's essential to acknowledge the person before getting down to business. Start any conversation, or enter any shop, by saying: *"Bonjour, madame (or monsieur)."* To ask if they speak English, say, *"Parlez-vous anglais?"*, and hope they speak more English than you speak French (most do). See "Survival Phrases" at the end of this chapter.

Money

France uses the euro currency: 1 euro (€) = about $1.10. To convert prices in euros to dollars, add about 10 percent: €20 = about $22, €50 = about $55. (Check www.oanda.com for the latest exchange rates.)

The standard way for travelers to get euros is to withdraw money from ATMs (which locals call a *distributeur*) using a debit or credit card, ideally with a Visa or MasterCard logo. Before departing, call your bank or credit-card company: Confirm that your card(s) will work overseas, ask about international transaction fees, and alert them that you'll be making withdrawals in Europe. Also ask for the PIN number for your credit card in case it'll help you use Europe's "chip-and-PIN" payment machines (see below); allow time for your bank to mail your PIN to you. To keep your valuables safe, wear a money belt.

Dealing with "Chip and PIN": Much of Europe—including France—is adopting a "chip-and-PIN" system for credit cards, and some merchants rely on it exclusively. European chip-and-PIN cards are embedded with an electronic chip, in addition to the magnetic stripe used on our American-style cards. This means that your credit (and debit) card might not work at payment machines, such as those at train and subway stations, toll roads, parking garages, luggage lockers, and self-serve gas pumps. Major US banks are beginning to offer credit cards with chips, but many of these are chip-and-signature cards, for which your signature (not your PIN) verifies your identity. In Europe, these cards should work for live transactions and at most payment machines, but probably won't work for offline transactions such as at unattended gas pumps. If a payment machine won't take your card, look for a machine that takes cash or see if there's a cashier nearby who can manually process your transaction. Often the easiest solution is to pay for your purchases with cash you've withdrawn from an ATM using your debit card (Europe's ATMs still accept magnetic-stripe cards).

Dynamic Currency Conversion: If merchants or hoteliers offer to convert your purchase price into dollars (called dynamic currency conversion, or DCC), refuse this "service." You'll pay more in fees for the expensive convenience of seeing your charge in dollars. If an ATM offers to "lock in" or "guarantee" your conversion rate, choose "proceed without conversion." Other prompts might state, "You can be charged in dollars: Press YES for dollars, NO for euros." Always choose the local currency.

Staying Connected

Smart travelers call ahead or go online to double-check tourist information, learn the latest on sights (special events, tour schedules, and so on), book tickets and tours, make reservations, reconfirm hotels, and research transportation connections.

To call France from the US or Canada: Dial 011-33 and then the local number, omitting the initial zero. (The 011 is our international access code, and 33 is France's country code.)

To call France from a European country: Dial 00-33 followed by the local number, omitting the initial zero. (The 00 is Europe's international access code.)

To call within France: Just dial the local number (including the initial zero).

To call from France to another country: Dial 00 followed by the country code (for example, 1 for the US or Canada), then the area code and number. If you're calling European countries whose phone numbers begin with 0, you'll usually have to omit that 0 when you dial.

Tips: Traveling with a mobile phone—whether an American one that works in France, or a European one you buy when you arrive—is handy, but can be pricey. If you bring your own phone, consider getting an international plan; most providers offer a global

From: rick@ricksteves.com
Sent: Today
To: info@hotelcentral.com
Subject: Reservation request for 19-22 July

Dear Hotel Central,

I would like to reserve a room for 2 people for 3 nights, arriving 19 July and departing 22 July. If possible, I would like a quiet room with a double bed and a bathroom inside the room.

Please let me know if you have a room available and the price.

Thank you!
Rick Steves

PRACTICALITIES

calling plan that cuts the per-minute cost of phone calls and texts, and a flat-fee data plan.

Use Wi-Fi whenever possible. Most hotels and many cafés offer free Wi-Fi, and you'll likely also find it at tourist information offices, major museums, and public-transit hubs. With Wi-Fi you can use your smartphone to make free or inexpensive domestic and international calls via a calling app such as Skype, FaceTime, or Google+ Hangouts. When you can't find Wi-Fi, you can use your cellular network to connect to the Internet, text, or make voice calls. When you're done, avoid further charges by manually switching off "data roaming" or "cellular data."

It's possible to stay connected without a mobile phone, but since French pay phones are being phased out, you'll need to use your hotel-room phone. To make cheap international calls from your hotel, you can buy an international phone card (*carte à code*; pronounced cart ah code). These work with a scratch-to-reveal PIN code, allow you to call home to the US for pennies a minute, and also work for domestic calls. Calling from your hotel-room phone without using an international phone card is usually expensive. For more on phoning, see www.ricksteves.com/phoning.

Making Hotel Reservations

I recommend reserving rooms in advance, particularly during peak season. For the best rates, book directly with the hotel using their official website (not a booking agency's site). If there's no secure reservation form, or for complicated requests, send an email with the following information: number and type of rooms; number of nights; arrival date; departure date; and any special requests. (For a sample email, see the sidebar.) Use the European style for writing dates: day/month/year. Hoteliers typically ask for your credit-card number as a deposit.

Some hotels are willing to deal to attract guests: Try emailing several hotels to ask for their best price. In general, hotel prices can soften if you do any of the following: offer to pay cash, stay at least three nights, or travel off-season.

The French have a simple hotel-rating system based on amenities (zero through five stars, indicated in this book by * through *****). Two-star hotels are my mainstay. Other accommodation options include bed-and-breakfasts (*chambres d'hôtes*, usually more affordable than hotels), hostels, campgrounds, or even homes (*gîtes*, rented by the week).

Eating

The cuisine is a highlight of any French adventure. It's sightseeing for your palate. For a formal meal, go to a restaurant. If you want the option of lighter fare (just soup or a sandwich), head for a café or brasserie instead.

French restaurants usually open for dinner at 19:00 and are typically most crowded around 20:30. Last seating is usually about 21:00 or 22:00 (earlier in villages). If a restaurant serves lunch, it generally goes from about 11:30 to 14:00.

In France, an entrée is the first course, and *le plat* or *le plat du jour* is the main course with vegetables. If you ask for the *menu* (muh-noo), you won't get a list of dishes; you'll get a fixed-price meal—usually your choice of three courses (soup, appetizer, or salad; main course with vegetables; and cheese course or dessert). Drinks are extra. Ask for *la carte* (lah kart) if you want to see a menu and order à la carte, like the locals do. Request the waiter's help in deciphering the French.

Cafés and brasseries provide budget-friendly meals. If you're hungry between lunch and dinner, when restaurants are closed, go to a brasserie, which generally serves throughout the day. (Some cafés do as well, but others close their kitchens from 14:00 to 18:00.) Compared to restaurants, cafés and brasseries usually have more limited and inexpensive fare, including salads, sandwiches, omelets, *plats du jour*, and more. Check the price list first, which by law must be posted prominently. There are two sets of prices: You'll pay more for the same drink if you're seated at a table (*salle*) than if you're seated or standing at the bar or counter (*comptoir*).

A 12-15 percent service charge (*service compris*) is always included in the bill. Most French never tip, but if you feel the service was exceptional, it's kind to tip up to 5 percent extra.

Transportation

By Train: Travelers who need to cover long distances in France by train can get a good deal with a France Railpass, sold only outside Europe. To see if a railpass could save you money, check www.rick

steves.com/rail. To research train schedules, visit Germany's excellent all-Europe website, www.bahn.com. The French rail website is www.sncf.com; for online sales, go to http://en.voyages-sncf.com. You can also buy tickets at train-station ticket windows, SNCF boutiques (small, centrally located offices of the national rail company), and travel agencies.

All **high-speed TGV trains** in France require a seat reservation—book as early as possible, as these trains fill fast, and some routes use TGV trains almost exclusively. This is especially true if you're traveling with a railpass, as TGV passholder reservations are limited, and usually sell out well before other seat reservations do.

You are required to validate (*composter*, kohm-poh-stay) all train tickets and reservations; before boarding look for a yellow machine to stamp your ticket or reservation. Strikes (*grève*) in France are common but generally last no longer than a day or two; ask your hotelier if one is coming.

By Car: It's cheaper to arrange most car rentals from the US. For tips on your insurance options, see www.ricksteves.com/cdw, and for route planning, consult www.viamichelin.com. Bring your driver's license.

Local road etiquette is similar to that in the US. Ask your car-rental company for details, or check the US State Department website (www.travel.state.gov, search for your country in the "Learn about your destination" box, then click on "Travel and Transportation").

France's toll road (*autoroute*) system is slick and speedy, but pricey; four hours of driving costs about €25 in tolls (pay cash, since US credit cards probably won't work in the machines). A car is a worthless headache in cities—park it safely (get tips from your hotel or pay to park at well-patrolled lots; look for blue *P* signs). As break-ins are common, be sure all of your valuables are out of sight and locked in the trunk, or even better, with you or in your hotel room.

Helpful Hints

Emergency Help: In France, dial 112 for any **emergency**. For English-speaking **police**, dial 17. To summon an **ambulance**, call 15. To replace a passport, call the **US Consulate and Embassy** in Paris (tel. 01 43 12 22 22, 4 Avenue Gabriel, Mo: Concorde, http://france.usembassy.gov) or the **US Consulate** in Marseille (tel. 01 43 12 47 54). Canadians can call the **Canadian Consulate and Embassy** in Paris (tel. 01 44 43 29 02, 35 Avenue Montaigne, Mo: Franklin D. Roosevelt, www.amb-canada.fr) or the **Canadian Consulate** in Nice (tel. 04 93 92 93 22). For other concerns, get advice from your hotelier.

Theft or Loss: France has hardworking pickpockets, and

they particularly target those coming in from Paris airports—wear a money belt. Assume beggars are pickpockets and any scuffle is simply a distraction by a team of thieves. If you stop for any commotion or show, put your hands in your pockets before someone else does.

To replace a passport, you'll need to go in person to an embassy or consulate (see above). Cancel and replace your credit and debit cards by calling these 24-hour US numbers collect: Visa—tel. 303/967-1096, MasterCard—tel. 636/722-7111, American Express—tel. 336/393-1111. In France, to make a collect call to the US, dial 08 00 90 06 24 and say "operator" for an English-speaking operator. File a police report either on the spot or within a day or two; you'll need it to submit an insurance claim for lost or stolen railpasses or travel gear, and it can help with replacing your passport or credit and debit cards. Precautionary measures can minimize the effects of loss—back up your digital photos and other files frequently. For more information, see www.ricksteves.com/help.

Time: France uses the 24-hour clock. It's the same through 12:00 noon, then keep going: 13:00, 14:00, and so on. France, like most of continental Europe, is six/nine hours ahead of the East/West Coasts of the US.

Business Hours: Most shops are open from Monday through Saturday (generally 10:00–12:00 & 14:00–19:00) and closed on Sunday, though some grocery stores, bakeries, and street markets are open Sunday morning until noon. In smaller towns, many businesses are closed on Monday until 14:00 and sometimes all day. Touristy shops are usually open daily.

Sights: Opening and closing hours of sights can change unexpectedly; confirm the latest times with the local tourist information office or its website. Some major churches enforce a modest dress code (no bare shoulders or shorts) for everyone, even children.

Holidays and Festivals: France celebrates many holidays, which can close sights and attract crowds (book hotel rooms ahead). For information on holidays and festivals, check France's website: http://us.rendezvousenfrance.com. For a simple list showing major—though not all—events, see www.ricksteves.com/festivals.

Numbers and Stumblers: What Americans call the second floor of a building is the first floor in Europe. Europeans write dates as day/month/year, so Christmas 2016 is 25/12/16. Commas are decimal points and vice versa—a dollar and a half is 1,50, a thousand is 1.000, and there are 5.280 feet in a mile. France uses the metric system: A kilogram is 2.2 pounds; a liter is about a quart; and a kilometer is six-tenths of a mile.

Resources from Rick Steves

This Snapshot guide is excerpted from my latest edition of *Rick Steves France*, which is one of more than 30 titles in my series of guidebooks on European travel. I also produce a public television series, *Rick Steves' Europe*, and a public radio show, *Travel with Rick Steves*. My website, www.ricksteves.com, offers free travel information, a forum for travelers' comments, guidebook updates, my travel blog, an online travel store, and information on European railpasses and our tours of Europe. If you're bringing a mobile device on your trip, you can download my free Rick Steves Audio Europe app, featuring podcasts of my radio shows, audio tours of major sights in Europe, and travel interviews about France. You can get Rick Steves Audio Europe via Apple's App Store, Google Play, or the Amazon Appstore. For more information, see www.ricksteves.com/audioeurope. You can also follow me on Facebook and Twitter.

Additional Resources

Tourist Information: http://us.rendezvousenfrance.com
Passports and Red Tape: www.travel.state.gov
Packing List: www.ricksteves.com/packing
Travel Insurance: www.ricksteves.com/insurance
Cheap Flights: www.kayak.com
Airplane Carry-on Restrictions: www.tsa.gov
Updates for This Book: www.ricksteves.com/update

How Was Your Trip?

If you'd like to share your tips, concerns, and discoveries after using this book, please fill out the survey at www.ricksteves.com/feedback. Thanks in advance—it helps a lot.

French Survival Phrases

When using the phonetics, try to nasalize the <u>n</u> sound.

English	French	Pronunciation
Good day.	*Bonjour.*	boh<u>n</u>-zhoor
Mrs. / Mr.	*Madame / Monsieur*	mah-dahm / muhs-yur
Do you speak English?	*Parlez-vous anglais?*	par-lay-voo ah<u>n</u>-glay
Yes. / No.	*Oui. / Non.*	wee / noh<u>n</u>
I understand.	*Je comprends.*	zhuh koh<u>n</u>-prah<u>n</u>
I don't understand.	*Je ne comprends pas.*	zhuh nuh koh<u>n</u>-prah<u>n</u> pah
Please.	*S'il vous plaît.*	see voo play
Thank you.	*Merci.*	mehr-see
I'm sorry.	*Désolé.*	day-zoh-lay
Excuse me.	*Pardon.*	par-doh<u>n</u>
(No) problem.	*(Pas de) problème.*	(pah duh) proh-blehm
It's good.	*C'est bon.*	say boh<u>n</u>
Goodbye.	*Au revoir.*	oh vwahr
one / two	*un / deux*	uh<u>n</u> / duh
three / four	*trois / quatre*	twah / kah-truh
five / six	*cinq / six*	sa<u>n</u>k / sees
seven / eight	*sept / huit*	seht / weet
nine / ten	*neuf / dix*	nuhf / dees
How much is it?	*Combien?*	koh<u>n</u>-bee-a<u>n</u>
Write it?	*Ecrivez?*	ay-kree-vay
Is it free?	*C'est gratuit?*	say grah-twee
Included?	*Inclus?*	a<u>n</u>-klew
Where can I buy / find...?	*Où puis-je acheter / trouver...?*	oo pwee-zhuh ah-shuh-tay / troo-vay
I'd like / We'd like...	*Je voudrais / Nous voudrions...*	zhuh voo-dray / noo voo-dree-oh<u>n</u>
...a room.	*...une chambre.*	ewn shah<u>n</u>-bruh
...a ticket to ___.	*...un billet pour ___.*	uh<u>n</u> bee-yay poor ___
Is it possible?	*C'est possible?*	say poh-see-bluh
Where is...?	*Où est...?*	oo ay
...the train station	*...la gare*	lah gar
...the bus station	*...la gare routière*	lah gar root-yehr
...tourist information	*...l'office du tourisme*	loh-fees dew too-reez-muh
Where are the toilets?	*Où sont les toilettes?*	oo soh<u>n</u> lay twah-leht
men	*hommes*	ohm
women	*dames*	dahm
left / right	*à gauche / à droite*	ah gohsh / ah dwaht
straight	*tout droit*	too dwah
When does this open / close?	*Ça ouvre / ferme à quelle heure?*	sah oo-vruh / fehrm ah kehl ur
At what time?	*À quelle heure?*	ah kehl ur
Just a moment.	*Un moment.*	uh<u>n</u> moh-mah<u>n</u>
now / soon / later	*maintenant / bientôt / plus tard*	ma<u>n</u>-tuh-nah<u>n</u> / bee-a<u>n</u>-toh / plew tar
today / tomorrow	*aujourd'hui / demain*	oh-zhoor-dwee / duh-ma<u>n</u>

In a French Restaurant

English	French	Pronunciation
I'd like / We'd like...	Je voudrais / Nous voudrions...	zhuh voo-dray / noo voo-dree-ohn
...to reserve...	...réserver...	ray-zehr-vay
...a table for one / two.	...une table pour un / deux.	ewn tah-bluh poor uhn / duh
Is this seat free?	C'est libre?	say lee-bruh
The menu (in English), please.	La carte (en anglais), s'il vous plaît.	lah kart (ahn ahn-glay) see voo play
service (not) included	service (non) compris	sehr-vees (nohn) kohn-pree
to go	à emporter	ah ahn-por-tay
with / without	avec / sans	ah-vehk / sahn
and / or	et / ou	ay / oo
special of the day	plat du jour	plah dew zhoor
specialty of the house	spécialité de la maison	spay-see-ah-lee-tay duh lah may-zohn
appetizers	hors d'oeuvre	or duh-vruh
first course (soup, salad)	entrée	ahn-tray
main course (meat, fish)	plat principal	plah pran-see-pahl
bread	pain	pan
cheese	fromage	froh-mahzh
sandwich	sandwich	sahnd-weech
soup	soupe	soop
salad	salade	sah-lahd
meat	viande	vee-ahnd
chicken	poulet	poo-lay
fish	poisson	pwah-sohn
seafood	fruits de mer	frwee duh mehr
fruit	fruit	frwee
vegetables	légumes	lay-gewm
dessert	dessert	day-sehr
mineral water	eau minérale	oh mee-nay-rahl
tap water	l'eau du robinet	loh dew roh-bee-nay
milk	lait	lay
(orange) juice	jus (d'orange)	zhew (doh-rahnzh)
coffee / tea	café / thé	kah-fay / tay
wine	vin	van
red / white	rouge / blanc	roozh / blahn
glass / bottle	verre / bouteille	vehr / boo-tay
beer	bière	bee-ehr
Cheers!	Santé!	sahn-tay
More. / Another.	Plus. / Un autre.	plew / uhn oh-truh
The same.	La même chose.	lah mehm shohz
The bill, please.	L'addition, s'il vous plaît.	lah-dee-see-ohn see voo play
Do you accept credit cards?	Vous prenez les cartes?	voo pruh-nay lay kart
tip	pourboire	poor-bwahr
Delicious!	Délicieux!	day-lee-see-uh

For more user-friendly French phrases, check out *Rick Steves' French Phrase Book and Dictionary* or *Rick Steves' French, Italian & German Phrase Book.*

INDEX

INDEX

INDEX

Explore Europe

At ricksteves.com you can browse through thousands of articles, videos, photos and radio interviews, plus find a wealth of money-saving travel tips for planning your dream trip. And with our mobile-friendly website, you can easily access all this great travel information anywhere you go.

TV Shows

Preview the places you'll visit by watching entire half-hour episodes of Rick Steves' Europe (choose from all 100 shows) on-demand, for free.

ricksteves.com

your travel dreams into affordable reality

Radio Interviews

Enjoy ready access to Rick's vast library of radio interviews covering travel

tips and cultural insights that relate specifically to your Europe travel plans.

Travel Forums

Learn, ask, share! Our online community of savvy travelers is a great resource for first-time travelers to Europe, as well as seasoned pros. You'll find forums on each country, plus travel tips and restaurant/hotel reviews. You can even ask one of our well-traveled staff to chime in with an opinion.

Travel News

Subscribe to our free Travel News e-newsletter, and get monthly updates from Rick on what's happening in Europe.

Audio Europe™

Rick's Free Travel App

Get your FREE **Rick Steves Audio Europe**™ app to enjoy...

- Dozens of self-guided tours of Europe's top museums, sights and historic walks
- Hundreds of tracks filled with cultural insights and sightseeing tips from Rick's radio interviews
- All organized into handy geographic playlists
- For iPhone, iPad, iPod Touch, Android

With Rick whispering in your ear, Europe gets even better.

Find out more at ricksteves.com

Pack Light and Right

Gear up for your next adventure at ricksteves.com

Light Luggage

Pack light and right with Rick Steves' affordable, custom-designed rolling carry-on bags, backpacks, day packs and shoulder bags.

Accessories

From packing cubes to moneybelts and beyond, Rick has personally selected the travel goodies that will help your trip go smoother.

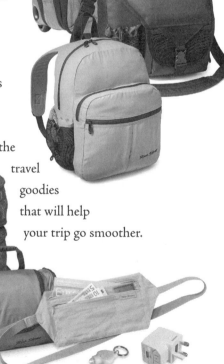

Shop at ricksteves.com

Rick Steves has

Experience maximum Europe

Save time and energy

This guidebook is your independent-travel toolkit. But for all it delivers, it's still up to you to devote the time and energy it takes to manage the preparation and logistics that are essential for a happy trip. If that's a hassle, there's a solution.

Rick Steves Tours

A Rick Steves tour takes you to Europe's most interesting places with great

great tours, too!

with minimum stress

guides and small groups of 28 or less. We follow Rick's favorite itineraries, ride in comfy buses, stay in family-run hotels, and bring you intimately close to the Europe you've traveled so far to see. Most importantly, we take away the logistical headaches so you can focus on the fun.

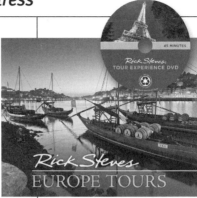

customers—along with us on 40 different itineraries, from Ireland to Italy to Istanbul. Is a Rick Steves tour the right fit for your travel dreams? Find out at ricksteves.com, where you can also get Rick's latest tour catalog and free Tour Experience DVD.

Join the fun

This year we'll take 18,000 free-spirited travelers— nearly half of them repeat

Europe is best experienced with happy travel partners. We hope you can join us.

See our itineraries at ricksteves.com

Rick Steves

Rick Steves guidebooks are published by Avalon Travel, a member of the Perseus Books Group

Maximize your travel skills
with a good guidebook.

AVEL CULTURE

rope 101
ropean Christmas
stcards from Europe
vel as a Political Act

OOKS

arly all Rick Steves guides are available as
ooks. Check with your favorite bookseller.

CK STEVES' EUROPE DVDs

New Shows 2015-2016
stria & the Alps
e Complete Collection 2000-2016
stern Europe
gland & Wales
ropean Christmas
ropean Travel Skills & Specials
ance
rmany, BeNeLux & More
eece, Turkey & Portugal
e Holy Land: Israelis & Palestinians Today
n
and & Scotland
ly's Cities
y's Countryside
andinavia
ain
vel Extras

PHRASE BOOKS & DICTIONARIES

French
French, Italian & German
German
Italian
Portuguese
Spanish

PLANNING MAPS

Britain, Ireland & London
Europe
France & Paris
Germany, Austria & Switzerland
Ireland
Italy
Spain & Portugal

Photo © Patricia Feaster

RickSteves.com @RickSteves

Rick Steves books are available at bookstores
and through online booksellers.

Avalon Travel
a member of the Perseus Books Group
1700 Fourth Street
Berkeley, California 94710

Printed in Canada by Friesens. First printing January 2016.

ISBN 978-1-63121-207-9

For the latest on Rick's lectures, guidebooks, tours, public radio show, and public television series, contact Rick Steves' Europe, 130 Fourth Avenue North, Edmonds, WA
98020, 425/771-8303, rick@ricksteves.com, www.ricksteves.com.

Rick Steves' Europe

Special Publications Manager: Risa Laib
Managing Editor: Jennifer Madison Davis
Editors: Glenn Eriksen, Tom Griffin, Katherine Gustafson, Suzanne Kotz, Cathy Lu,
  John Pierce, Carrie Shepherd
Editorial & Production Assistant: Jessica Shaw
Editorial Intern: Chelsea Wing
Researchers: Mary Bouron, Tom Griffin, Cameron Hewitt, Kristen Michel, Virginie
  Moré
Contributor: Gene Openshaw
Maps & Graphics: David C. Hoerlein, Sandra Hundacker, Lauren Mills, Mary Rostad

Avalon Travel

Senior Editor and Series Manager: Madhu Prasher
Editor: Jamie Andrade
Associate Editors: Maggie Ryan, Sierra Machado
Copy Editors: Judith Brown and Rebecca Freed
Proofreader: Kelly Lydick
Indexer: Beatrice Wikander
Production & Typesetting: Tabitha Lahr, Rue Flaherty, Christine DeLorenzo
Cover Design: Kimberly Glyder Design
Maps & Graphics: Kat Bennett, Mike Morgenfeld

Photo Credits

Front Cover: Abbey of Mont St-Michel, Normandy, France © Yulia Kuznetsova /
  Alamy Stock Photo
Title Page: Pont du Hoc, Battlefield in WW2 during the invasion of Normandy ©
  mizio1970/www.123rf.com
Additional Photography: Dominic Arizona Bonuccelli, Abe Bringolf, Mary Ann
  Cameron, Julie Coen, Rich Earl, Barb Geisler, Cameron Hewitt, David C. Hoerlein,
  Michaelanne Jerome, Lauren Mills, Virginie Moré, Gene Openshaw, Paul Orcutt,
  Rhonda Pelikan, Michael Potter, Carol Ries, Steve Smith, Robyn Stencil, Rick
  Steves, Gretchen Strauch, Rob Unck, Laura VanDeventer, Dorian Yates, Wikimedia
  Commons (PD-Art/PD-US0). Photos are used by permission and are the property
  of the original copyright owners.

ABOUT THE AUTHORS

RICK STEVES

Since 1973, Rick Steves has spent 100 days every year exploring Europe. Along with writing and researching a best-selling series of guidebooks, Rick produces a public television series *(Rick Steves' Europe),* a public radio show *(Travel with Rick Steves),* a blog (on Facebook), and an app and podcast *(Rick Steves Audio Europe);* writes a nationally syndicated newspaper column; organizes guided tours that take over 20,000 travelers to Europe annually; and offers an information-packed website (www.ricksteves.com). With the help of his hardworking staff of 100 at Rick Steves' Europe—in Edmonds, Washington, just north of Seattle—Rick's mission is to make European travel fun, affordable, and culturally enlightening for Americans.

Connect with Rick:

 facebook.com/RickSteves twitter: @RickSteves
 instagram: ricksteveseurope

STEVE SMITH

Steve Smith manages tour guides for the Rick Steves' Europe tour program and has been researching guidebooks with Rick for over two decades. Fluent in French, he's lived in France on several occasions, starting when he was seven. Steve owns a restored farmhouse in rural Burgundy where he hangs his beret in research season. Steve's wife, Karen Lewis Smith—an expert on French cuisine and wine—provides invaluable contributions to his books.

Want more France?
Maximize the experience with Rick Steves as your guide

Guidebooks
Provence and Paris guides make side-trips smooth and affordable

Phrase Books
Rely on Rick's French Phrase Book & Dictionary

Rick's TV Shows
Preview your destinations with 12 shows on France

Free! Rick's Audio Europe™ App
Get free audio tours for Paris' top sights

Small Group Tours
Rick offers several great itineraries through France

For all the details, visit ricksteves.com